2030 NOW
17 GOALS, 9 BILLION PEOPLE, 1 FUTURE

Previous pages:

Salt evaporation ponds of Lake Mariut, Alexandria, Alexandria Governorate, Egypt (31° 7′ 8.06″ N – 29° 49′ 44.78″ E).

Elephants in the swamplands of the Okavango Delta, Botswana (19° 25′ S – 23° 14′ E).

Market near the neighborhood of Xochimilco, Mexico City, Mexico (19 °27′ N – 99° 16′ W).

Our heartfelt thanks to all of the 2030 NOW ambassadors, artists, scientists and local heroes, and to everyone else whose commitment and knowledge helped to make this book possible.

2030 NOW

Editors: Stine Trier Norden and Søren Rud

Concept: Life Exhibitions

Initiated by: Torben Wind

Author: Susanne Sayers

Art Director: Christian Kirk-Jensen / Danish Pastry Design

Photo Editor: Vibeke Højgaard Frederiksen

Global Strategy: Anne Line Hansen

Scientific Editor: Michael Helt Knudsen

Research: Poul Arnedal

Translation: Tam McTurk, Ashley Douglas and Matt Evans of Citadel Translations, Scotland

Art Presented by: ART 2030 - www.art2030.org

ART-2030
CONNECTING ART &
THE UN GLOBAL GOALS

2030 NOW

17 GOALS, 9 BILLION PEOPLE, 1 FUTURE

LIFE
PUBLISHING

FOREWORD

BAN KI-MOON, THE EIGHTH SECRETARY-GENERAL OF THE UNITED NATIONS, UN

On a brisk Sunday morning in 2009, I was among many who gathered in Copenhagen to see an outdoor exhibition of photographs that captured breathtaking landscapes from across the planet. Panel after panel, everyone quietly grasped the solemn meaning of the exhibition: *100 Places to Remember Before They Disappear*.

In Spring of 2014, I visited the town of Ilulissat, Greenland, just a short distance away from the North Pole.

The majestic beauty of the land was thrilling. The seemingly inevitable fate of its eventual disappearance was overwhelming.

These experiences were transformative.

The 2030 NOW project harnesses the extraordinarily transformative power of Yann Arthus-Bertrand's photographs with equally forceful stories of local activists and globally renowned figures to advance the cause of the United Nation's 17 Sustainable Development Goals.

Adopted by 193 member-states back in 2015, these goals provide the world with a collaborative blueprint to ensure *The Future We Want* – a just, equitable, and inclusive world for generations to come.

I consider the 2030 Agenda one of the proudest achievements of my career in public service and welcome all opportunities to lend my support towards its success. I have no doubt in my mind that it represents our best chance to preserve the one and the only planet that we inhabit.

Within these pages, you will find – just as I had many years ago – a powerful and passionate plea for compassion and action.

I hope it will open your eyes to the dire realities of today and inspire you to be part of shaping a brighter tomorrow.

Sandbanks on the coast of Whitsunday Island, Queensland, Australia (20° 15′ S – 149° 01′ E).

THINK, CR

SUSANNE SAYERS, AUTHOR

If a utopia is a vision of a bright future that has not yet come to pass, then the United Nations 2030 Sustainable Development Goals (UN 2030 Goals) might be described as precisely that. Jan Eliasson, former Deputy Secretary General of the UN, points out in this book that the goals might more accurately be called a survival kit for humanity – a sat-nav leading us toward a sustainable future in which nearly 9 billion people peacefully coexist without depleting Earth's natural resources.

Nor are the goals utopian in the sense of wishful but unrealistic thinking. All UN member states back them, and a wide range of experts see good reason for hope rather than despair – despite the fact that far too many people still suffer the consequences of hunger, poverty, war and oppression, and that we continue to wipe out species and flirt with climate disaster. Considerable progress has already been made toward achieving the goals by 2030, a point driven home by many of the contributors to the book, including Canadian psychology professor and author Steven Pinker and Google futurist Ray Kurzweil.

The consensus is that the goals are attainable, and that everybody has a role to play. This book portrays some of the many people who are working hard to make the world a better place for others. At first, we referred to them as "local heroes". In truth, they are more than that. They are action heroes. They persist in fighting and defying seemingly impossible odds, even when all looks lost and the prospects of success seem tiny. Some of them are well known, including on the international stage. Others are active at the local level and are more or less unknown outside of their own communities. They are all inspiring figures and demonstrate that everyone has a role to play – we just have to act.

Our action heroes are young and old, poor and billionaires. They are housewives, students, entrepreneurs, scientists and business people. What unites them is a burning desire to make a difference, to make the world a better and brighter place.

The book also presents 17 ambassadors – public figures who use their status to raise awareness of the UN 2030 Goals. It showcases our wonderful, wild, stunning, rugged and awe-inspiring planet, as captured through the lens of world-renowned photographer Yann Arthus-Bertrand.

We also tell the stories of 17 artists who invite us to see the world in new ways. They encourage us to dream,

EATE, ACT

to think big and to pose the question that has always been the key to progress: "What if…?"

If we can imagine something, we can make it happen. Maybe not right here and now, but sooner or later.

Sick pay, pensions, holidays and free health care were once considered utopian. Nowadays, they are either already a basic right in many parts of the world or they soon will be. People dared to think, to fight and to make these dreams come true.

Although the book explores the 17 UN 2030 Goals one by one, they are in fact connected at a very fundamental level – so much so that the UN portrays them as a virtuous circle. Action that prevents climate change helps to eliminate hunger and poverty, protect life on land and at sea, improve human health and make our cities good places to live. Improving education creates conditions that nurture equality, reduce poverty and spread tolerance and peace. Together, the goals all point toward a single objective: a better future for all living things on Earth.

We are already making significant progress. Every single day, more than 130,000 people are lifted out of extreme poverty. Every single day, medical science becomes more effective at preventing and treating disease. Every single day, education reaches more children than ever before, electricity reaches more homes, more of us have access to knowledge and more of us have enough to eat.

Our vision for 2030 is of a world in which no one is left behind. But we will only get there if we dare to ask: "What if…?", and dare to act – all of us. The South African activist Koketso Moeti says that our actions don't need to be spectacular – being part of the struggle for a better future can be as simple as helping a neighbour or providing food or childcare to those who need it.

It is our sincere hope that 2030 NOW will inspire and encourage people to do their bit. Big or small, it doesn't matter – every little counts. Even if we don't achieve every single one of the 17 goals by 2030, each and every contribution takes us one step further away from utopia and one step closer to reality.

THINK, CREATE, ACT!

A LIFE OF DIGNITY ON A LIVING PLANET

The UN 2030 Goals represent the most ambitious global agenda ever devised. Adopted unanimously by the member states in 2015, the 17 goals plot a path toward a future in which nobody is left behind and everyone lives a life of dignity. A future in which we use resources in a sustainable manner and preserve the vibrancy and diversity of the natural world. A future in which climate change and environmental destruction have been reversed.

What makes the 2030 agenda unique is that it covers the whole world – every country and every person on Earth. – unlike the 2015 Millennium Development Goals, which were adopted at the turn of the century and focused on the developing world.

The 17 goals are inextricably interlinked, and are often depicted as a circle. It is impossible to achieve any one of them in isolation – progress toward one invariably entails some degree of progress toward another.

A number of specific targets have been set for each of the goals – 169 in total. The targets clearly set out what we, as leaders, politicians, citizens, organisations and companies must strive to achieve. Each chapter in the book summarises the targets in the form of a vision for the goal.

Only when all 169 targets have been reached for all of us, everywhere on Earth, will it be possible to say that we have achieved the future we want so much.

Read more at: sustainable.un.org

END POVERTY IN ALL ITS FORMS EVERYWHERE.
P.18

END HUNGER, ACHIEVE FOOD SECURITY AND IMPROVED NUTRITION, AND PROMOTE SUSTAINABLE AGRICULTURE.
P.34

ENSURE ACCESS TO AFFORDABLE, RELIABLE, SUSTAINABLE, AND MODERN ENERGY FOR ALL.
P.114

PROMOTE SUSTAINED, INCLUSIVE AND SUSTAINABLE ECONOMIC GROWTH, FULL AND PRODUCTIVE EMPLOYMENT AND DECENT WORK FOR ALL.
P.130

TAKE URGENT ACTION TO COMBAT CLIMATE CHANGE AND ITS IMPACTS (IN LINE WITH THE UNITED NATIONS FRAMEWORK CONVENTION ON CLIMATE CHANGE).
P.210

CONSERVE AND SUSTAINABLY USE THE OCEANS, SEAS AND MARINE RESOURCES FOR SUSTAINABLE DEVELOPMENT.
P.226

ENSURE HEALTHY LIVES
AND PROMOTE
WELL-BEING FOR ALL
AT ALL AGES.
P.50

ENSURE INCLUSIVE
AND EQUITABLE QUALITY
EDUCATION AND
PROMOTE
LIFE-LONG LEARNING
OPPORTUNITIES FOR
ALL.
P.66

ACHIEVE GENDER
EQUALITY AND EMPOWER
ALL WOMEN AND GIRLS.
P.82

ENSURE AVAILABILITY
AND SUSTAINABLE
MANAGEMENT OF WATER
AND SANITATION
FOR ALL.
> P.98

BUILD RESILIENT
INFRASTRUCTURE,
PROMOTE INCLUSIVE
AND SUSTAINABLE
INDUSTRIALIZATION
AND FOSTER
INNOVATION.
P.146

REDUCE INEQUALITY
WITHIN AND AMONG
COUNTRIES.
P.162

MAKE CITIES AND
HUMAN SETTLEMENTS
INCLUSIVE, SAFE,
RESILIENT AND
SUSTAINABLE.
P.178

ENSURE SUSTAINABLE
CONSUMPTION AND
PRODUCTION PATTERNS.
P.194

PROTECT, RESTORE AND
PROMOTE SUSTAINABLE
USE OF TERRESTRIAL
ECOSYSTEMS,
SUSTAINABLY MANAGE
FORESTS, COMBAT
DESERTIFICATION, AND
HALT AND REVERSE LAND
DEGRADATION AND HALT
BIODIVERSITY LOSS.
P.242

PROMOTE PEACEFUL AND
INCLUSIVE SOCIETIES
FOR SUSTAINABLE
DEVELOPMENT,
PROVIDE ACCESS TO
JUSTICE FOR ALL AND
BUILD EFFECTIVE,
ACCOUNTABLE AND
INCLUSIVE INSTITUTIONS
AT ALL LEVELS.
P.258

STRENGTHEN
THE MEANS OF
IMPLEMENTATION
AND REVITALIZE THE
GLOBAL PARTNERSHIP
FOR SUSTAINABLE
DEVELOPMENT.
P.274

CONTENTS

GOAL 01

NO POVERTY

"I'M NOT AFRAID OF EMOTIONS.

I met children with empty eyes. They do not play or smile. They lost feeling because of hunger, torture, lack of care, verbal and physical abuse, and rape. They are truly 'the wretched of the earth'. Nobody notices those children. They are non-existent in the eyes of society because most of them don't have official papers that confirm their existence. Most of them don't know how old they are. They have never celebrated their birthdays. I want to talk about the lives of these children. I can no longer live my life without feeling what other people are suffering"

NADINE LABAKI

Actor and director of the award-winning film *Capernaum*

Previous double page: Killick Stenio Vincent, Jalousie, Petionville, Port-au-Prince district, Haiti
(18° 30' 39.25" N – 72° 17' 41.41" W)

GOAL 01
END POVERTY IN ALL ITS FORMS EVERYWHERE

- -

The vision: By 2030, extreme poverty will be eradicated. The proportion of men, women and children of all ages living in poverty will be reduced by at least half. All men and women will have equal rights to economic resources, access to basic services, new technologies and financial services, and ownership and control over land and other forms of property. The poor and the vulnerable will have substantial social protection that enables them to cope with extreme events resulting from climate change, conflicts and other economic, social and environmental shocks and disasters

IN 1987,
35%
OF THE WORLD
POPULATION LIVED IN
EXTREME POVERTY.
IN SUB-SAHARAN
AFRICA IT WAS
54%

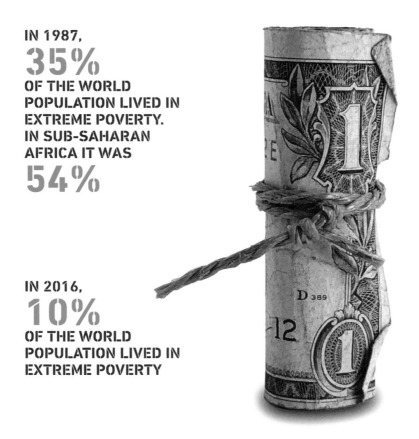

IN 2016,
10%
OF THE WORLD
POPULATION LIVED IN
EXTREME POVERTY

... HOWEVER,
IN 2016,
43%
OF THE POPULATION
IN SUB-SAHARAN
AFRICA STILL
SUBSISTS ON LESS
THAN
$1.90
PER DAY
(THE UN-APPROVED
POVERTY THRESHOLD)

(**Source:** World Inequality Lab:
World Inequality Report 2018)

WALKING WITHOUT SHAME

Africa and South-east Asia have the worst levels of extreme poverty in the world. Despite a global drop of 50% since 1990, nearly every fifth child in the developing world is still raised in a household that subsists on less than $1.90 per day. In sub-Saharan Africa, it is every second child. Poverty not only severely impedes the physical and mental development of individual young people, but it also causes great harm to the societies in which they grow up.

While billions of people still teeter on the brink of extreme poverty, many more face lives of relative poverty, with incomes far below the national average, struggling to play a full part in society. Nor is child poverty confined to the developing countries. In some of the wealthiest parts of the world, as many as one in five children do not have enough to eat.

Even short periods of poverty can have a life-long impact, and not just in financial terms. One British study revealed that three-year-olds from poorer families lagged nine months behind their more affluent peers in development terms, a gap that widens throughout childhood.

Poor pupils generally fare worse at school. They can't afford to take part in the same activities as their better-off classmates. They are more susceptible to poor health, homelessness, social exclusion and depression. All of this perpetuates the poverty gap, making it more likely that they will remain poor in adult life.

Feelings of inferiority and guilt are another common side-effect of poverty. Adam Smith, the Scottish social philosopher, economist and author of *The Wealth of Nations*, wrote that being poor meant not having what was needed to walk in public without shame. New studies reaffirm that poverty is still very much associated with this negative emotion.

The first of the UN 2030 Goals is not just about eradicating extreme poverty, it is about working to end it in all its forms everywhere, and giving everybody the chance to participate fully in their society without shame.

01. CREATE
KARA WALKER

"CHALLENGING AND HIGHLIGHTING ABUSIVE POWER DYNAMICS IN OUR CULTURE IS MY GOAL; REPLICATING THEM IS NOT"

Growing up in California in the 1970s, Kara Walker didn't dwell much on her origins. She lived in a liberal, free-thinking state and her parents were respected members of society. One of her earliest memories is of watching her artist father draw, and deciding, "I want to be an artist too."

She was 13 when her family left the milder climate – in all senses – of California and moved to Atlanta Georgia, in the heartlands of the South with its history of plantations and slavery. Suddenly, she found herself categorised as a person of colour and defined as such.

"There is a moment when you go from subject to object and I guess that was my moment," explains Walker.

"I think of California as a golden diverse kind of period, which is not entirely true. But certainly in Georgia, in high school, things were very locked down into black and white. You were forced to determine your allegiance."

Walker has spent much of her career exploring themes of race, gender, inequality, power, exploitation and how that connects to poverty. She is perhaps best known for her large-scale paper silhouettes, which tell the stories of slaves and their lives in the southern states. They may look like the kind of delicate paper cut-outs made by middle-class ladies as a genteel pastime, but hers are brutal, sexualised images that confront head-on themes of oppression, subjugation and the relationship between slave and owner, black and white.

Her sculpture of a boy with a banana basket is made of sugar and was originally part of the large installation *A Subtlety*, which was put on display in a disused sugar factory. The centrepiece was a huge, glittering sphinx, with the face of a typical slave woman from the South. It is a striking reference to the sugar industry, which generated massive wealth for plantation owners, while the slaves were worked to death to produce "white gold". In Walker's work, poverty and injustice cannot be separated.

"Sugar crystallises something in our American soul. It is emblematic of all industrial processes, and of the idea of becoming white – white being equated with pure and 'true'. It takes a lot of energy to turn brown things into white things. A lot of pressure."

KARA WALKER

New York-based artist, best known for her candid investigation of race, gender, sexuality, and violence. **Artworks:** *African Boy Attendant Curio*, 2014. Next page: *A Sublety*, 2014.

01. THINK
THE OPTIMISTS HAVE
THE FACTS ON THEIR SIDE

"THE UN SUSTAINABLE DEVELOPMENT GOALS ARE NOT JUST SOME UTOPIAN DREAM – IN FACT, QUITE THE CONTRARY", STEVEN PINKER

Have you ever seen the headline "130,000 escaped extreme poverty today" splashed across your newspaper? Almost certainly not. And yet, while poverty undeniably remains a global problem, the number of people living in extreme poverty has fallen by more than 130,000 per day over the last three decades.

It's not the only good news either. In the long term, the overall trend in human prosperity is a steady upward curve. Temporary setbacks notwithstanding, the world is a much better place in general than it was 50 years ago, never mind 100 or 200 years ago.

In his books, talks and interviews, Professor Pinker has pointed out this progress and backed it up with facts. Living conditions are improving dramatically, and the UN 2030 Goals are within reach – not within easy reach, but neither are they, as he puts it, "Pollyanna fantasies invented by people singing Kumbaya around the campfire".

"The goals are highly tangible, achievable, and backed by all UN member states," he says. "And they are proof that nations can agree on the value and the rights of humanity without sharing nationality or religion. We do not need a sense of nationalism or a common

STEVEN PINKER

Canadian-American cognitive psychologist and author of bestsellers such as *The Better Angels of Our Nature* and *Enlightenment Now: The Case for Reason, Science, Humanism and Progress.*

religion to recognise what should be a better future for all, or to respect the well-being of the individual."

Despite all this, the vision of a better future is frequently met with scepticism. As an expert in human nature, Pinker believes this reflects a partially innate human trait – we tend to be on the lookout for potential threats rather than opportunities. He also notes that critics are usually considered smart and sophisticated,

The lively nightlife in many African cities, as here in Windhoek, Namibia, is a sign that poverty is declining.

optimists naïve. "But when it comes to the progress of humanity, the optimists have the facts on their side. They are the hard-headed realists, whereas the pessimists actually live in a state of delusion," he says.

Let's look at the facts. Even though some of the numbers are estimates, the trends are reliable.

Over the last century, the global average life expectancy at birth has more than doubled, according to economist Max Roser's online magazine *Our World in Data*. It is now 72 years. Today, even the lowest national figure, which is just below 53 years, is higher than the highest life expectancy in any region in 1800.

Around 200 years ago, just around half of all children lived beyond their fifth birthday. Today, 96% reach that milestone.

When it comes to literacy and education, in the early 1800s only 12% could read and write. Today, 85% of the global population is literate, and the same proportion has at least a basic education. As for freedom and empowerment, more than half of the world's population live in democracies. Two centuries ago, that figure was 1%. Colonial rule has all but

disappeared in the last 50 years, too, with former colonies now being independent nations or largely self-governing constituent contries.

The cost of products and services that enable us to live better lives and educate ourselves has dropped drastically. Pinker mentions as an example the almost unimaginable fall in the cost of artificial lighting, which enables us to study and read outside of normal daylight hours.

In the early 19th century, the cost of an hour's worth of light from a tallow candle was equivalent to around six hours of hard graft for the average person. In 1950, this had dropped to eight seconds of work for much-improved light from an electric bulb. Today, the equivalent cost would be in microseconds. Similarly, most of us now have way more processing power in our smartphones than all of NASA's computers combined at the time of its first manned mission to the Moon and back.

Globally, the proportion of people living in extreme poverty is now almost down to 10%, from 90% two centuries ago, according to the World Bank and measured in terms of purchasing power, household surveys and obtainable data.

So why do we tend to believe things are getting worse? Pinker notes that news media are not well suited to presenting positive stories.

"The media are concerned with sudden changes, and usually changes for the worse. Progress doesn't happen on a Thursday in October, it is a long process. A sudden onset of a crisis, even if it is small or brief, will usually gain a lot more attention than even radical progress," Pinker explains.

In spite of global improvements, Pinker warns that progress is not something to be taken for granted. He is deeply worried that the Age of Enlightenment, which has brought unprecedented improvement over the last 300 years, is now under attack. Reason and science have been sidetracked and obscured, while junk science, alarmist viewpoints, populist notions based on raw emotions and the demonisation of large groups of people are gaining traction.

"Progress can be approached in two different versions: As overcoming struggles and evil forces, or as solving problems. Sometimes it is necessary to defeat evil forces – World War II is an example. But today there is a political tendency on both the Left and Right to point out groups of people and label them evil forces. That can be counterproductive, and it certainly is not synonymous with progress."

Pinker thinks that the UN goals are approaching progress from the correct angle: as problems to be solved, be it climate change, poverty, hunger, responsible consumption or clean energy. Humans are experts at problem-solving, and our technological innovations have enabled us to develop a much better understanding of how problems are interconnected and the tools we need to solve them, including education.

"This really is the key to achieving most of the goals," says Pinker. "Somebody who gets an education is much more likely to avoid poverty and starvation, to live long, and avoid disease. Societies that put emphasis on education are much more likely to be democratic and they harbour less aggression. Education is a vindication of Enlightenment, and the UN 2030 Goals are founded in that ideal. The fact that the world's nations came together to adopt them is uplifting and inspiring."

AN ALTERNATIVE TO MONEY UNDER THE MATTRESS

They can't put money in the bank, they can't save up safely or accumulate interest on their savings, and they can't get insurance. Over two billion adults of working age don't have access to the financial services that the rest of the world takes for granted.

One of the reasons is that many of the world's poorest and most isolated people simply live so far from the nearest bank that it's practically impossible to use it.

The concept of financial inclusion has arrived on the agenda in recent years – advancing the attempts to provide the world's poorest and most vulnerable access to savings, credit, insurance and financial advice.

The trend towards digitalisation of the economy and financial services offers an opportunity to bring savings out from under the proverbial mattress. Digital transfers let people save and make payments without the risks associated with reliance on hard cash. Microfinance – which is tailor-made for really small economies – continues to spread and become digital, and the level of demand for it proves that the need is huge.

In Bangladesh, approximately a quarter of the adult population are now customers of the mobile bank bKash, established in 2011. It offers a fast, cheap, and secure way of transferring money, and the vast majority of the population, who don't live within easy reach of a bank branch, can use it.

In Ghana, the digital network company Tigo has developed a range of financial services specifically aimed at the poorest section of the population, including a life insurance policy with monthly payments that has doubled the insurance market in Ghana and means many more people are now covered.

Digital financial inclusion has the potential to make the financial position of the world's poorest people more secure and make them less vulnerable as individuals, but a broader approach is required to ensure that they are also in a position to understand both the opportunities and their rights.

In the mountains of Nepal a grandmother is taking care of her grandchild. Around the world, many elderly people contribute to their society in numerous ways, even when they are no longer working.

THE FINANCIAL FRAILTY OF THE ELDERLY

In some parts of the world, people look forward to their old age – or at least to the life of a pensioner – with good savings and plenty of free time to travel, care for grandkids, hang out with friends and indulge in their favourite pastimes.

For many others, the outlook is far less rosy – people with no pension would find themselves entirely dependent on friends and family if they were to fall ill or lose the ability to support themselves. In most parts of the world, the traditional pattern of inter-generational living and younger people looking after their older relatives is on the wane. Millions of people have been left in a precarious position, often compounded by age discrimination and a lack of any recognition of the contribution they have made to society.

In 2015, there were around 900 million people aged 60 or over. By 2030, according to UN forecasts, that number will have reached 1.4 billion, and account for almost 17% of the world's population. All of the indications suggest that figure will continue to rise.

In 2016, almost one-third of elderly people in the world had no pension, but the global average conceals huge regional disparities. In sub-Saharan Africa, the proportion of older people without any form of pension soars to 80%. Women are particularly vulnerable – partly because they live longer on average, and partly because they have often spent their lives working in the home and have not had the chance to save up.

All of these older people contribute to society around the world in countless – often unrecognised – ways. They act as childminders and carers for their spouses and family, they are full of valuable knowledge and experience, and those who remain in good health often undertake voluntary work that benefits society as a whole. The challenge is to ensure not only that they have a secure income, but also that they are included, appreciated and afforded the same opportunities as everyone else to play an active role in society.

01. ACT
LIFELONG STRUGGLE AGAINST POVERTY

AVANILDO DUQUE, PROJECT COORDINATOR FOR THE NGO "ACTIONAID", WORKING FOR SOCIAL JUSTICE, GENDER EQUALITY AND AN END TO POVERTY

For Duque, education became a route out of poverty, albeit not an obvious one, as it wasn't an opportunity open to many from his part of the country.

"Even as a kid, I had a sense of justice and an understanding of the social inequalities that affected my family. I also knew that education would improve our quality of life, including for the future generations," he says.

Today, Duque is the campaign manager for NGO ActionAid in Brazil, but his activism started when he was studying agricultural science.

"Student movements were highly politicised at the time and filled in the gaps in our education not covered by the curriculum. They made us aware of things like agricultural reforms, the rights of landless workers, and modern cultivation methods that excluded peasant farmers and used chemicals that are harmful to people and the environment," explains Duque.

"I realised that it wasn't enough just to fight for better living conditions for me and my loved ones. I had to use my skills to fight for the sort of profound change that would affect wider society and improve life for the poor and excluded."

The struggle against poverty and inequality still plays a key role in Duque's life, and he focuses on women's rights and opportunities. "In Brazil and across the world, women are worst affected by poverty and find it hardest to escape its clutches," he says.

"Inequality is still rife when it comes to access to politics, power and money. Patriarchal violence has led to a culture in which women don't have power over their bodies and sexuality, but we have gradually increased their awareness of their rights, and progress is being made in terms of influence in the family and society as well."

In 2017, his advocacy of women's rights saw him awarded the title of "He for She" by *Claudia* magazine, which also lauded him for his promotion of gay and transgender rights. His work for ActionAid also involves campaigns for better education for all. One of the NGO's major success stories was the approval of a national education plan and better funding for education.

However, not everything is moving in the right direction. Duque explains that although Brazil had begun to make considerable progress in lifting people out of poverty and promoting greater economic justice, these trends have reversed in recent years.

Nevertheless, he is optimistic and hopes that the UN 2030 Goals will be achieved both locally and globally.

"By the time we reach 2030, I hope that we will see greater economic equality and fewer refugees, that we will take better care of the environment, and that discrimination will be consigned to the dustbin of history. But to achieve all that we will need to work more closely together."

Avanildo Duque has battled poverty and injustice most of his life.

GOAL 02

- -

ZERO HUNGER

- -

"NO ONE SHOULD GO TO BED HUNGRY.
But nearly 780 million people in developing regions
are undernourished. Finding a permanent end to hunger
remains a major challenge. Where so many of us take our
daily routine of eating for granted, a large proportion of the
people on this planet struggle to feed themselves and their
families. No one should wonder where their next meal is
coming from. Everyone on this planet deserves and should
have daily access to nutritious food. Unfortunately, that is not
the world we live in today. Reducing world hunger cannot be
solved with one simple solution. But the UN's Zero Hunger
Challenge seeks to focus on the problem. Let's ensure that
all people across the globe have food. It will take a collective
effort in working together to end hunger and malnutrition.
Join me in making this possible by 2030"

ZOE SALDANA

Activist and actor, UN Women Champion for Innovation

Previous double page: Woman fishing with a net on the delta, south of Padmapukur, Khulna district, Bangladesh
(22° 15' 58.86" N – 89° 11' 42.63" E)

GOAL 02
END HUNGER, ACHIEVE FOOD SECURITY AND IMPROVED NUTRITION, AND PROMOTE SUSTAINABLE AGRICULTURE

The vision: By 2030, hunger will be ended, and all people will have access to safe, nutritious and sufficient food all year round. Malnutrition, including stunting and wasting in small children, will be a thing of the past. Agriculture productivity and the income of small-scale farmers and producers will be doubled. We will have resilient agricultural practices that are not only efficient but also help to maintain ecosystems and strengthen the capacity for adaption to climate change and extreme weather. Trade restrictions will be lifted, and all forms of agricultural export subsidies will be eliminated

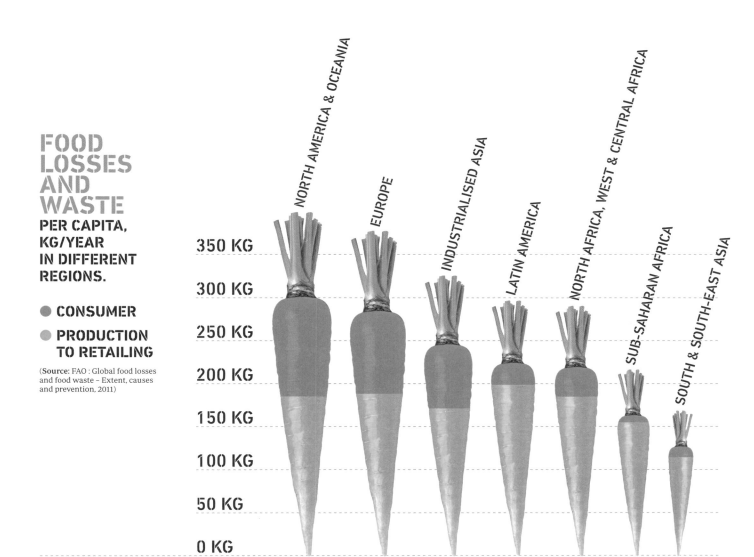

FOOD LOSSES AND WASTE

PER CAPITA, KG/YEAR IN DIFFERENT REGIONS.

● CONSUMER
● PRODUCTION TO RETAILING

(**Source:** FAO : Global food losses and food waste – Extent, causes and prevention, 2011)

350 KG
300 KG
250 KG
200 KG
150 KG
100 KG
50 KG
0 KG

NORTH AMERICA & OCEANIA
EUROPE
INDUSTRIALISED ASIA
LATIN AMERICA
NORTH AFRICA, WEST & CENTRAL AFRICA
SUB-SAHARAN AFRICA
SOUTH & SOUTH-EAST ASIA

FOOD FOR ALL

In the ten seconds or so it takes to read this sentence, the world will produce 1,268 tons of food, of which 856 tons will be eaten and 412 discarded.

Massive efficiency gains in food production over the last three decades have halved the number of people who do not have enough to eat. In fact, we produce far more than we need – enough to feed almost 10 billion people, the projected global population in 2050.

Despite this progress, one in nine people has insufficient food to lead an active and healthy life. The problem is not a lack of food, but the uneven way it is distributed. More people now die from obesity than hunger, but statistically malnutrition – whether triggered by lack of nutrition, or a calorie intake that is too low or too high – affects every second person on the planet. Obesity is a particular concern in developing countries, where traditional meals based on local produce are being replaced by highly processed, mass-produced food and the physical labour of farms and many industries is giving way to sedentary, desk-based jobs.

Natural disasters, extreme weather events, and conflicts such as those in Syria and Sudan demonstrate only too clearly how rapidly the local picture can deteriorate, leading to severe hunger in areas that would have plenty of food under normal circumstances. One third of the food we produce also goes to waste – destroyed in the fields or just after harvest, spoiled en route to markets and shops, disposed of unsold or thrown out by consumers because it was past its use by date and because we just could not eat it all.

Ending hunger by 2030 will require concerted action in a number of areas. As things stand at the moment, a combination of poverty, disaster, war, overworked land, inefficient farming methods, lack of water, lack of labour, inadequate markets, poor transport and unsafe roads means that malnutrition and hunger are still destroying the futures of millions of people.

The food is there. The challenge is ensuring that everyone eats a healthy, nutritious, high-quality diet based on high-quality produce. And that nobody eats so much that they become ill or die as a result.

02. CREATE
RIRKRIT TIRAVANIJA,
NIKOLAUS HIRSCH, MICHEL MÜLLER

"I AM NOT INTERESTED IN AUTHORSHIP; I AM INTERESTED IN THE POSSIBILITIES THAT CAN BE ARRIVED AT WHEN PEOPLE PUT THEIR IDEAS TOGETHER"

At first glance, the bamboo pavilion of *DO WE DREAM UNDER THE SAME SKY* resembles a crude open-air kitchen – and indeed, it is precisely that. But it is also much more. It is part of artist Rirkrit Tiravanija's ongoing exploration of collaboration, social relations and sustainability.

Cooking and eating together are among the most basic forms of human interaction. When we eat together, we share stories, beliefs, thoughts and ideas. *DO WE DREAM UNDER THE SAME SKY* invites guests and artists to cook together in parabolic solar ovens, using ingredients from local producers and fragrant basil, thyme, mint, rosemary and hyssop from the pavilion's own herbal garden.

Tiravanija created the installation along with architects Nikolaus Hirsch and Michel Müller. It is a place to share meals and food for thought. The interactions are the real work of art.

Sharing ideas, knowledge and experiences are at the heart of all Tiravanija's projects. In 1992, he turned a New York gallery into a kitchen and invited the guests to cook and dine. His collaborative project *The Land*, in the Thai province of Chiang Mai, transformed a plot of land into a Utopian community and artistic

RIRKRIT TIRAVANIJA

Contemporary artist born in Buenos Aires residing in New York City, Berlin, Chiang Mai. **Artworks:** Rirkrit Tiravanija, Nikolaus Hirsch, Michel Müller, Antto Melasniemi: *DO WE DREAM UNDER THE SAME SKY*, Art Basel, Switzerland 2015. Next page: Rirkrit Tiravanija, Nikolaus Hirsch, Michel Müller: *DO WE DREAM UNDER THE SAME SKY*, Aarhus 2017.

refuge. Rooted in principles of self-sufficiency and sustainability, the project sought to balance innovation and tradition.

Eventually, the open-air kitchen and dining areas from *DO WE DREAM UNDER THE SAME SKY* will be incorporated into *The Land*, alongside structures by other artists and architects. The gradually evolving community draws inspiration from the Surrealist "exquisite corpse game" – the elements are all by different people, which often makes the outcomes surprising and invites new social interactions.

02. THINK
REVOLUTIONISING AFRICA BY MOBILE PHONE

NEW AND BETTER CROPS, AGRICULTURAL ADVICE, MARKET PRICES, DROUGHT WARNINGS, HELP WITH DRAWING UP CONTRACTS – ALL BY TEXT MESSAGE. THE MOBILE PHONE IS ALREADY HELPING AFRICAN FARMERS GROW MORE AND BETTER FOOD, BUT MOBILE TECHNOLOGY HAS SO MUCH MORE TO OFFER

In the Nakuru district, north-west of the Kenyan capital Nairobi, Fred has a problem. His cattle are eating soil, and he can't figure out why, or if he should be worried. He gets out his mobile and texts a local number belonging to the network WeFarm: "My cattle are eating earth. Anybody have any idea why?" Within minutes, a farmer in Vihiga, a couple of hundred kilometres away, responds: "They're probably lacking important minerals in their diet."

WeFarm uses a simple app to connect about 700,000 farmers in Kenya and Uganda, who help each other across vast distances, without the need for smartphones or internet access. Instead, text messages are sent to local numbers and then shared automatically with the whole network. Replies are sent out the same way.

Since it was launched in 2015, WeFarm members have posted over 800,000 questions and received more than 1.2 million answers. They discuss problems, solutions and ideas, and more than a third of them contribute several times a month. Farmers often live in isolated areas with no internet access, so many have found it enormously helpful to have somewhere to turn for advice.

WeFarm is just one example of how the mobile phone is providing much-needed support for food production in Africa. In raw numbers, more people go hungry in Asia, but the proportion of the population is higher in Africa – one in four sub-Saharan Africans is undernourished. With mobile phone ownership rapidly increasing, technology provides opportunities for people to band together and improve this situation. New networks and apps improve conditions for farmers and other small-scale producers by giving them faster and easier access to important information.

Several African countries have price-monitoring apps and services that inform farmers about local market prices and where demand is highest. This cuts down on wasted trips to markets only to find prices are too low or that their produce is unsellable and has to be thrown out.

Mobile phones are giving people more opportunities to get good prices for their catch and produce, like here outside the fish market in Angoche, Mozambique, and to arrange deals before going to the market.

Some services convert text messages into audible speech, which is invaluable in areas where much of the population is still illiterate. Others allow farmers and customers to negotiate and agree to purchases in advance – again, saving time and preventing food waste.

In Kenya, a number of agricultural associations have come together to launch the Mbegu Choice service, which spreads knowledge about new and better crops, especially grain varieties.

New crops are often better and more stable than the old ones, but in countries where communities are separated from each other by huge distances and poor roads, it is difficult to get the message across. The service encourages farmers to try out different types of crops. This not only makes farms less vulnerable to scavenging animals and plant disease, but also means that more types of produce are available on the market.

Limited diet and lack of nutrition are problems in many parts of Africa. Teaching farmers what grows well and why it's a good idea to change crops is good for variety and for food security.

Technology already allows us to monitor the risk of drought, right down to local level, providing an early-warning system for farmers and others. The system combines satellite surveillance with observations from people on the ground, who submit information online. It also lets farmers with drought insurance document losses of crops and animals, making it quicker and easier to submit a claim.

These examples only scratch the surface of what technology has to offer.

One of the biggest challenges is that relatively few Africans – and the poor people of the world in general – have acces to the internet. Mobile broadband and easier access to energy – especially solar and wind power – will facilitate better and quicker internet coverage, even in isolated areas. People will also be able to summon help when needed, e.g. in the wake of a natural disaster.

Sensors and drones will be able to monitor fields and water levels. In times of conflict, they will be able to identify which areas are in the greatest need, which are easiest to reach, and which should be avoided. Drones will deliver emergency aid to areas that are otherwise inaccessible.

The first priorities, however, are better food security and reducing crop losses. The mobile phone helps spread knowledge and information, which is a positive first step.

Back in Kenya, Clara, a single mother with five children, has used her mobile to increase her income. Last year, one of her cows was sick and the milk yield from another was low. She was worried. The cows were her only source of income. When the cow had been sick for three days, Clara asked a question on WeFarm.

Ten minutes later, another member responded. The same thing had happened to his cows, because their feed contained insufficient nutrients.

He told her what feed to use and which nutrients the cows needed. Another member confirmed this and advised Clara to grow silage crops, which would provide better nutrition for her cows. It worked – both animals are in fine fettle again and producing enough milk for Clara to sell to her neighbours and earn more money.

STOP WASTING FOOD

Wasted food is a huge problem. You can help solve it by being conscious of how to avoid food waste. It will also save you money.

• **USE THE FOOD YOU HAVE – ALL OF IT.** Try a weekly empty fridge day, when you use up all of the leftovers. This will also save you time and money on a trip to the supermarket.

• **PLAN YOUR SHOPPING AND MEALS.** If you have roast chicken today, how about a chicken salad with lots of vegetables tomorrow, or chicken soup?

• **GET TO GRIPS WITH THE REAL SHELF LIFE OF DIFFERENT FOODS.** Best before dates don't mean food will make you ill the very next day. A lot of it can be used past the sell-by date, e.g. slightly wilted fruit and vegetables in soups, stews or purees.

• **MORE TIPS AND ADVICE ARE AVAILABLE AT:** stopwastingfoodmovement.org

DISH OF THE DAY: BACTERIA

The ability to map DNA has led to breakthroughs in our knowledge of bacteria and underlined the critical importance of our own microbiota – the bacteria in our digestive system – to both our physical and mental health.

The research is still at an early stage, but growing interest in the importance of bacteria has already raised awareness of how important they are to plant health as well. In fact, they are so crucial that increasing numbers of companies and research institutions are working on ways of adding beneficial bacteria to seeds, providing them with an enriched packed lunch, as it were. Experiments show that this significantly enhances crop yield and disease resistance.

Attention is also being paid to the actual soil itself, as opposed to the crops. If the microorganism content of the soil is sufficiently high and healthy, fertilisers and pesticides become more or less redundant, and it can also hold more CO_2.

In traditional agriculture, the soil is ploughed, and then seeds are sown. But ploughing destroys many of the microorganisms in the ground, hence the need for fertilisers. By continually regenerating the microorganisms and carbon content, crop yields improve without the cost of fertilisers and pesticides.

The method requires minimal cultivation (no ploughing), varied crops and frequent seed changes. Many scientists believe that focusing on soil quality, rather than simply on crops in isolation, offers one of the most promising ways to boost food production without degrading the land.

A farewell to farms: Cherry tree and cow, Bessenay area, Monts du Lyonnais, Rhône, France (20° 15' S – 149° 01' E).

A FAREWELL TO FARMS?

Agriculture has developed significantly and production methods have changed several times during human history. The ultra-efficient, industrial methods of today have advantages, but one of the oldest forms – agroforestry – is enjoying a resurgence.

As the name suggests, trees play an important role. Instead of clearing them to make room for grazing, or for growing grain and other crops, forests are left untouched. Crops are cultivated in the shade of the trees, animals graze in the woods, eating grass, leaves, branches, nuts, roots and whatever else they can get their teeth into.

It may sound inefficient, but multiple studies and trials have confirmed that it is a sustainable method of farming that increases yields, prevents landslides and land degradation, cuts down on the use of chemicals and makes agriculture more resistant to disease, pests, droughts and floods.

The trees provide a valuable source of shade for crops. The plants don't need to be watered as often and are protected from harsh sunlight. The leaves provide nutrients to the soil, and the roots mean there is a high level of microorganisms in the ground.

Agroforestry usually involves cultivating multiple crops, which reduces the risk of hunger and under-nourishment if a particular crop fails.

Combining forestry with animal husbandry also has benefits for the health of both animals and trees. Animals fertilise the soil naturally and benefit from plenty of nutrients in return. Agroforestry has also been found to be far more effective at sequestering greenhouse gases from animals and storing them in the soil.

Project Drawdown ranks silvopasture (the combination of animal husbandry and forestry) as one of the top 10 most effective solutions to global warming. It is an effective way of reducing CO_2 emissions and improving agricultural yields and the robustness of the crops, making it a good overall investment. Silvopasture systems are also far richer in biodiversity than traditional fields or grazing areas.

02. ACT
THE WOMAN WHO TRANSFORMED A NATION'S FOOD CULTURE

RUSSIAN-BORN **SELINA JUUL** MOVED TO DENMARK AS A TEENAGER, SWAPPING A CHILDHOOD OF SCARCITY FOR A WORLD OF ABUNDANCE. WHEN IT ALL BECAME TOO MUCH FOR HER, SHE STARTED A MOVEMENT AGAINST FOOD WASTE

She might speak at 100 miles per hour, but Selina Juul certainly isn't all talk and no action. Quite the opposite. In the decade since she launched the Stop Wasting Food movement, she has significantly altered the thinking of Danish supermarkets and producers, as well as ordinary people in kitchens and at dining tables across the country.

Danes now throw out 14,000 tons less food waste p.a. than they did in 2011 – a per capita reduction of 8%. Supermarket chains have also changed how they sell food to cut down on waste.

Juul was born in Moscow. When she moved to Denmark aged 13, she didn't speak a word of the language and was completely unprepared for the sheer volume of food in the shops.

"It was quite a shock! I grew up in Moscow, where food was rationed. It was like gold. But in Denmark, there was more than enough of it. My classmates would toss their packed lunches in the bin, and I just didn't get it. How could they? When I asked, they just laughed," she recalls.

Food waste is taken seriously now. It has worked its way into consumer consciousness and onto the international political agenda. The UN aims to halve global food waste by 2030. Juul, who was voted "Dane of the Year 2014" for her work, is a global ambassador for the UN 2030 agenda on reducing food waste. She may be one of the world's most prominent food waste activists, but you won't find Selina rummaging around in bins and skips.

"The real focus is to eliminate the need to throw food away; to organise production so that we only make what people will eat and nothing goes to waste," she says. "We have to stop the waste long before the food ends up in any bin."

One billion people go to bed hungry while we throw away enough food to feed three billion. We all have to play a part if we are to alter this sorry state of affairs.

"Don't wait for others to solve the problem. Do something about it yourself. We're all consumers, and that makes us all part of both the problem and the solution."

Selina Juul has been the primary driver against food waste, talking to politicians, organisations, retailers and customers and changing attitudes and wasteful practices. Here she is among the key note speakers at the Nordic Business Forum 2017.

GOAL 03

- -

GOOD HEALTH AND WELL-BEING

- -

"MENTAL ILLNESS IS A GLOBAL CRISIS THAT MUST BE ADDRESSED.

It is the burden of populations; the challenge of governments and health systems; it's a family's heartbreak; and an individual's valiant struggle. The stigma and discrimination that prevents people from seeking help must be eliminated. Mental illness is the last frontier in civil rights. Why aren't we talking about an illness that affects one in four people?
I almost lost my sister and nephew because our family had no vocabulary for mental health issues and never talked about it! I co-founded Bring Change to Mind in 2010 to bring home a very loud message — remove the stigma around any form of mental illness, empower those who live with it, and those who love them, to acknowledge it, to talk about it, to get help and to eventually lead open and productive lives"

GLENN CLOSE
Co-founder, Bring Change to Mind

Previous double page: Blue Lagoon, near Grindavik, Reykjanes Peninsula, Iceland
(63° 54' N – 22° 25' W)

GOAL 03
ENSURE HEALTHY LIVES AND PROMOTE WELL-BEING FOR ALL

The vision: By 2030, the preventable deaths of newborns and children under five years of age will be a thing of the past, and maternal deaths will be rare. Epidemics such as tuberculosis, AIDS, malaria and neglected tropical diseases will be eliminated. There will be far fewer premature deaths from both communicable and non-communicable diseases, abuse and harmful chemicals and poisons in our environment. The number of deaths from traffic accidents will be halved. Everyone will have access to healthcare and to safe, effective and affordable essential medicines and vaccines

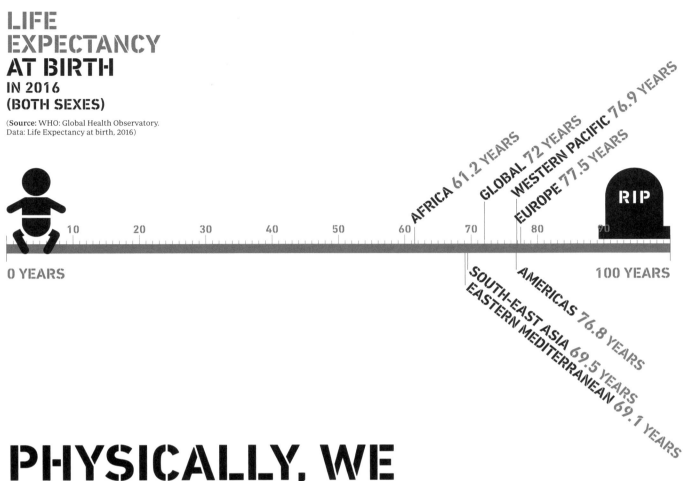

LIFE EXPECTANCY AT BIRTH
IN 2016
(BOTH SEXES)

(**Source:** WHO: Global Health Observatory.
Data: Life Expectancy at birth, 2016)

AFRICA 61.2 YEARS
GLOBAL 72 YEARS
WESTERN PACIFIC 76.9 YEARS
EUROPE 77.5 YEARS

RIP

0 YEARS
100 YEARS

SOUTH-EAST ASIA 69.5 YEARS
AMERICAS 76.8 YEARS
EASTERN MEDITERRANEAN 69.1 YEARS

PHYSICALLY, WE ARE MUCH HEALTHIER – BUT WHAT ABOUT MENTALLY?

There is no shortage of good news on the health front. Average global life expectancy is up 23 years since World War II. Maternal and infant mortality are down. Cures and preventative measures have eradicated a number of serious diseases, and greater access to clean water is helping to curb deadly outbreaks of cholera.

Although levels of inequality remain high, and many societies are still too poor to provide adequate health care and medicine, significant progress has been made – especially in sub-Saharan Africa, the part of the world hardest hit by the AIDS epidemic. HIV-inhibiting drugs have dramatically increased life expectancy, which is not just good for those infected, but also their children, who benefit from parental care for far longer.

However, the number of people suffering from mental health problems has increased during the same period, and far less attention is paid to the issue. Globally, one in four people are affected by mental and neurological diseases at some point in their lives. More than 300 million people suffer from depression, almost as many struggle with severe anxiety, and more than 800,000 commit suicide each year.

Far from being the "first-world problem" it was long assumed to be, depression is widespread in the developing countries – so much so that the World Health Organisation (WHO) has designated it the most common cause of disability. Unfortunately, in many parts of the world, mental illness is taboo or shrouded in myth, and millions of people do not receive the help they need.

Mental health is not just a medical issue. According to the WHO, economic disadvantage, inequality and social exclusion are all closely linked. We need to focus on the root causes as well as treating individual problems. Failure to address mental health will make it impossible to achieve the 2030 goal of health and well-being for all.

03. CREATE
JEPPE HEIN

"LIFE BEGINS WITH AN INHALE, AND ENDS WITH AN EXHALE. IN-BETWEEN WE ALL BREATHE DIFFERENT LIVES. AND YET, EACH BREATH KEEPS US TOGETHER, CONNECTED, SHARING THE SAME AIR"

A surprise can take our breath away. We take a breather when we need time to think. We breathe deeply when recovering from a shock. We breathe sighs of relief, we lose our breath when tired. We take a deep breath before we start to sing.

The language we use connects our soul, our very spirit, with breathing. When we are afraid, our lungs feel contracted into a tight knot, rendering us virtually incapable of breathing. All human life is based on breathing. When we have trouble with it – physically and mentally – we fall ill. Air pollution, anxiety and depression stop us from breathing freely.

In *Breathing Watercolours,* the Danish artist Jeppe Hein explores his breath. He has painted his own breath in long brush strokes – one for inhalation, one for exhalation. Long lines, blue as an unpolluted sky, gradually filling the space, almost as if the wall itself is breathing.

Hein came up with the idea while recovering from a breakdown. He noticed that his breathing was shallow and frenetic. He was inhaling and exhaling in short bursts. Gradually, he was able to take deeper, longer and calmer breaths – to inhale, hold, exhale, inhale, hold, exhale ... breathing became a lifeline. Painting his breath also made him more aware of how important it is to be able to breathe freely, to be able to enjoy a breath of fresh air, to have breathing space. Something that is taken for granted by many of us, but not an option for so many others.

JEPPE HEIN

Danish artist whose installations and sculptures play with our sensory experiences and invite the audience to take an active role. **Artworks:** *Appearing Rooms,* part of *Please Touch the Art,* NY, USA 2015. Next page: Jeppe Hein painting *Breathing Watercolours,* Norway 2016.

Hein's art reflects on and let us feel what is important in life. What is needed to open up people's hearts?

His accessible water pavilions offer both a physical experience and the opportunity for active participation to the public. They stimulate multiple reactions from joy and curiosity to doubt, wonder and surprise. This "liquid architecture" can be considered as a social sculpture playfully inserted into everyday life situations.

Hein thinks that what we need is to understand each other much more, especially with how the world is right now. "We need empathy. Perhaps we should have an 18th goal for 2030: Empathy".

03. THINK
"AN ARTIFICIAL ARM AND SOME GENE REPAIR, PLEASE!"

MEDICAL SCIENCE IS DEVELOPING RAPIDLY. THIS IS A GLIMPSE INTO THE FUTURE AND SOME OF THE PROMISING TECHNOLOGIES THAT COULD OFFER US BETTER HEALTH

At the moment, about 500,000 people around the world are aged 100 or over. By 2030, the number will have more than doubled. By 2050, it will be about 3.7 million and some 425 million people will be 80 or over.

Life expectancy is increasing rapidly all over the world. Indeed, some scientists even think a form of immortality is within reach. Others disagree, but science doesn't stand still. The list of diseases that we can either keep in check or cure completely gets longer and longer all the time. The same applies to the list of problems we are able to prevent, diagnose and treat accurately.

Here are just some of the technologies expected to make us healthier and improve our lives.

01. THE MOST KNOWLEDGEABLE DOCTOR IN THE WORLD

Every five years, the amount of information we have about medicine and diseases doubles. Old truths are frequently found not to hold, but while new knowledge provides new opportunities, it also poses challenges for doctors and health professionals, who may have difficulty keeping up and passing on the benefits of all this innovation to their patients.

This is where IBM's Watson comes in. Originally built to win at *Jeopardy*, the supercomputer has read millions of patient records, medical journals, medical studies, textbooks ... the whole body of knowledge out there, with new discoveries added every day.

"Doctor" Watson is a form of self-teaching artificial intelligence (AI) capable of processing plain language texts and unstructured data. Hopes are high that in the long term this kind of AI will make diagnoses more accurate.

Watson is better than any human doctor at keeping up to date and at spotting difficult-to-detect patterns and correlations. Unlike a human, Watson never has bad days and is never exhausted after a long shift. Having said that – and even though cancer clinics already use "Doctor" Watson to suggest the best treatment for individual patients based on their personal data – medical technology is still in its infancy.

Seven-year-old Faith Lennox grasps a toy with her new left hand, created by a 3D printer. Her forearm and hand were amputated when she was an infant after circulation to her limb was cut off during labour.

02. PRINTING SPARE PARTS FOR HUMANS

3D printing is one technology that has already made a difference. First invented some 30 years ago, the technology is now mature enough to print customised new teeth and crowns more effectively, less expensively and using fewer materials than previous methods. The same goes for artificial limbs. Individually customised arms and legs can be printed without huge costs to either the patient or the health service.

It may sound as if considerable progress has already been made, but the prospects for the future are even more impressive. Researchers in South Korea have already 3D-printed "bio-blood vessels" that work in animal experiments. In the future, 3D-printed organs such as skin, blood vessels and hearts may help us address the lack of organ donors.

The technology could also make it easier for the many people, especially older ones, who take several tablets a day and struggle with it. 3D printing is already being used to make pills that contain three different

medicines in one. The materials are designed to release the dosage into the body at specific times. This type of pill could be particularly useful for diabetes patients.

Thanks to 3D printing, the surgeons of the future will also be able to practise on organs that are artificial yet almost indistinguishable from the real thing.

03. FAREWELL TO STANDARD TREATMENTS

Chemotherapy works for some people. Not for others. Unfortunately, it is difficult to predict how individuals will respond to the treatment, so patients often endure serious side effects in vain.

Up until now, there has not been much doctors can do about it, but experts now predict that in future medicine will be administered in a way that is completely tailored to the individual patient, instead of standard treatments based on averages.

The Human Genome Project, which finished mapping the human genome in 2003, has played a huge role in

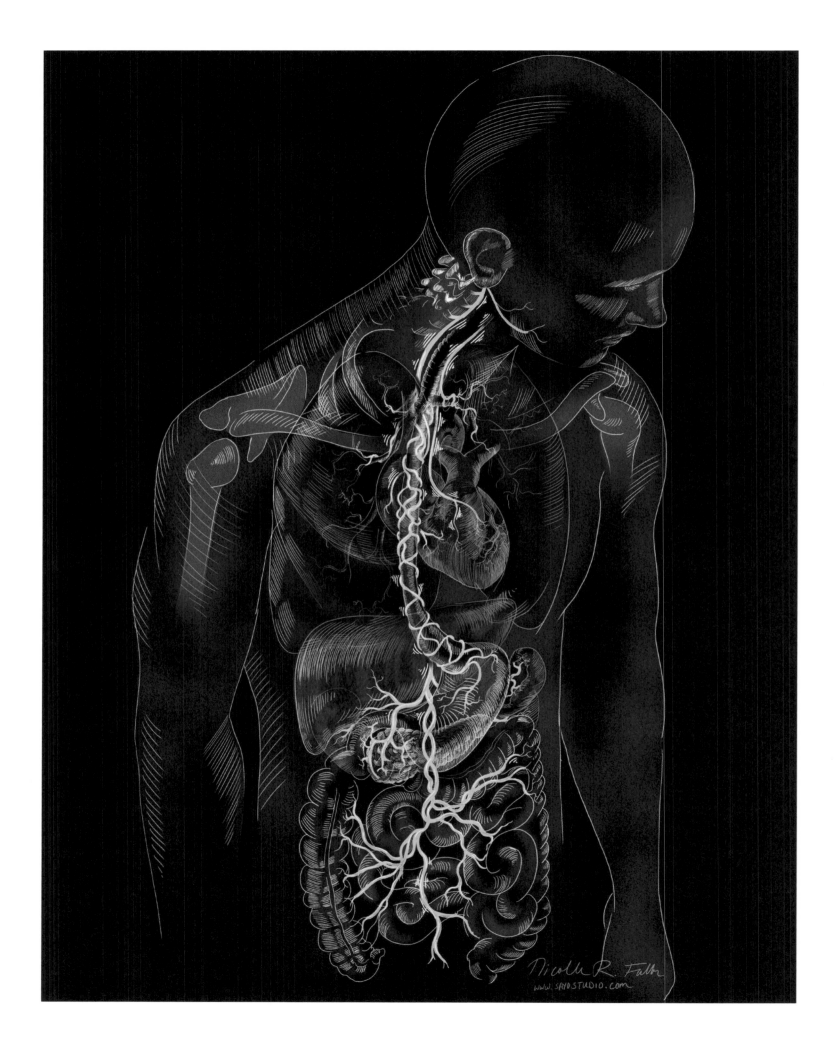

helping scientists better understand what will work on individual patients. The unique nature of our genetic material, or DNA, is one of the reasons why people react differently to the same treatment. The more data we have, the better we will be at predicting what treatment will have the best results with the fewest side effects.

The price of mapping an individual's genome is falling rapidly. It cost around $100,000 in the 2000s, but by 2025 it will only cost a dollar, according to the US government's National Human Genome Research Institute. This will make it cheap – maybe even natural – for doctors to order complete DNA profiles and base preventative measures, diagnoses and treatments on them. Mapping has also brought us closer to being able to use gene therapy (replacing damaged genes) on individuals.

04. TELEMEDICINE AND SELF-MONITORING

Self-monitoring is already a thing. Fitness devices tell us how many steps we've taken, how many calories we've burned and how we are sleeping. Telemedicine trials have also been a success all over the world, with patients using digital technology to keep in touch with their doctor or nurse and monitor and report on things like blood pressure, blood sugar or lung function. One of the benefits is that patients with the pulmonary condition COPD avoid unnecessary time spent in hospital.

Although it would depend on how far we are willing to share our health data, it isn't unthinkable that digital devices could send data to the ambulance service, for example. In theory, if the body is allowed to digitally transmit information that a heart attack or a blood clot is on the way, an ambulance could be there before you even know you need it.

05. A BRAIN IN THE STOMACH

The ability to map the human genome, the advent of supercomputers and the ability to process vast amounts of data, have allowed scientists to develop a far greater understanding of both the uniqueness and the importance of the bacteria in our digestive systems. In fact, because the digestive system controls so much of the body's hormone factory, some researchers even refer to the intestines as our second brain.

The Vagus Nerve innervates the heart, lungs and digestive tract, and is thought to play a vital role in the communication between our microbiota, guts and brain.

Our microbiota – the entire ecosystem of bacteria, fungi and other microorganisms – is such an essential element of our health, moods and personality that some researchers go as far as to say that it no longer makes sense to talk about an "I". In reality, each of us is a "we", a collection of trillions of bacteria plus the rest of the body. We contain over 1,000 different bacterial species, two-thirds of which are unique to the individual.

Research suggests a close correlation between the composition of our microbiota and a range of diseases and conditions, raising hopes that transplanting either bacteria or perhaps the substances that they produce, from one person to another might help prevent conditions such as obesity – and increasing our intake of beneficial bacteria could perhaps improve both our physical and mental health. The fact that our microbiota is so individual also gives rise to the hope that it holds the key to better and more accurate treatment based on microorganisms. On the other hand, scientists stress that there is a long way to go and that many of the correlations between bacteria, the body and the psyche remain unclear.

06. MICROSCOPIC SUBMARINES IN THE BODY

In the 1966 film *Fantastic Voyage*, a man has a blood clot. To save him, a submarine crew is shrunk to microscopic size and sent on a mission inside his body to remove the clot.

What was science fiction in 1966 is reality now – well, apart from the bit about shrinking people. The first nanobots, or microscopic robots, have been successfully used to target cancer cells in the bodies of mice. The robots are as small as a red blood cell, making them too small for any kind of engine, chip or other standard methods of propulsion. Instead, DNA material is charged with blood-clotting drugs. It also includes a special molecule that targets a particular protein found only in large quantities on the surface of tumor cells. Once the nanobots reach the tumors, they release the coagulant and cut off the blood supply to the cells, effectively suffocating them.

Nanobots also reach parts of the body other technologies don't reach. They hold the potential to deliver medicine with great precision, expand blood vessels and, in general, act as a sort of in-built disease-fighting army that provides back-up to your own immune system.

03. ACT
INDOMITABLE DOCTOR IN WAR-TORN SOUTH SUDAN

DR. EVAN ATAR ADAHA OPERATES UNDER ALMOST IMPOSSIBLE CONDITIONS IN SOUTH SUDAN. CIVIL WAR RAGES ALL AROUND BUT HE REFUSES TO GIVE UP, AND THE GOOD DOCTOR HAS SAVED THOUSANDS OF LIVES, ACCORDING TO THE UN REFUGEE AGENCY (UNHCR)

When South Sudan became the world's newest nation in 2011, it had just 120 doctors and 100 nurses for a population of 12 million. It has even fewer now. Many fled or have been killed during the civil war that has convulsed the young nation since 2013, claiming about 400,000 lives and forcing some four million people into exile. Conditions are so dire that nobody knows the exact numbers.

The situation in what remains of South Sudan's health service is just as bleak. The entire Upper Nile state, a vast area, is served by just one hospital, where Atar and his team can't even rely on their generator. The medical equipment also malfunctions frequently and is difficult to replace or repair.

Despite these trying circumstances, the doctor and his team perform around 60 operations a week and treat thousands of people a year. He often works 48-hour shifts and sees his wife and children, who live in Kenya, just three times a year.

Much of Atar's life has been defined by war. He was born and raised in Torit, in what is now South Sudan, and studied medicine in Khartoum, the capital of what was then the unified state of Sudan. After graduating, he started his career in Egypt but returned as a volunteer when violence broke out in Sudan, opening his first clinic in Kurmuk in 1997.

Conditions were difficult, and air strikes not uncommon. In 2011, Atar and his staff were forced to flee to the south, taking as much equipment as possible with them. After a month on the road, they finally set up a clinic in the new nation.

When not performing surgery, Dr Atar trains new nurses and midwives. Despite the seemingly insurmountable challenges, he refuses to give up. He believes that everyone has the right to treatment, irrespective of ethnicity, gender, nationality or role in the conflict.

"Nothing gives me greater pleasure than when my work eases someone's suffering or saves a life," he says.

Evan Atar, the UNHCR 2018 Nansen Refugee Award winner, in his surgery in South Sudan.

GOAL 04

- -

QUALITY EDUCATION

- -

"PEOPLE LOVE TO SAY,
'Give a man a fish, and he'll eat for a day.
Teach a man to fish, and he'll eat for a lifetime.'
– What they don't say is, 'And it would be nice
if you gave him a fishing rod.'
That's the part of the analogy that's missing"

TREVOR NOAH
Comedian, writer, television host

Previous double page: School in Hagadera camp, Daadab, Garissa County, Kenya
(0° 0' 0.39" S – 40° 21' 52.99" E)

GOAL 04
ENSURE INCLUSIVE AND EQUITABLE HIGH-QUALITY EDUCATION AND PROMOTE LIFELONG LEARNING OPPORTUNITIES FOR ALL

The vision: By 2030, all girls and boys should complete free, equitable and quality primary and secondary education. All women and men should have access to affordable and quality technical, vocational and tertiary education, including university. And many more people should have relevant skills for employment, decent jobs and entrepreneurship. All young people and most adults, both men and women, should be literate and numerate. And all should have the knowledge and skills needed to promote sustainable development and a culture of peace, equality and global citizenship

SCHOOL'S OVER

GLOBALLY, **36,3%** OF YOUNG PEOPLE HAVE LEFT SCHOOL BY THE TIME THEY REACH UPPER-SECONDARY AGE, MOST IN SUB-SAHARAN AFRICA.

(**Source:** UNESCO: Fact Sheet no. 48, February 2018)

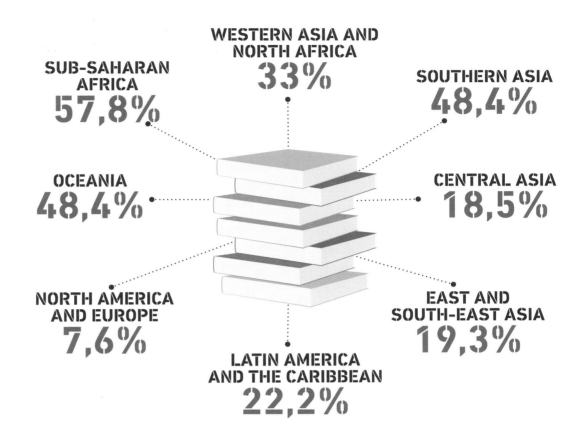

SUB-SAHARAN AFRICA 57,8%

WESTERN ASIA AND NORTH AFRICA 33%

SOUTHERN ASIA 48,4%

OCEANIA 48,4%

CENTRAL ASIA 18,5%

NORTH AMERICA AND EUROPE 7,6%

EAST AND SOUTH-EAST ASIA 19,3%

LATIN AMERICA AND THE CARIBBEAN 22,2%

THE WORLD IS CHANGING – WHAT ABOUT SCHOOLS?

What is it important to learn in school? Reading, writing and arithmetic? History? Geography? Religion? What about climate change, human rights, computer programming, digital skills, democratic engagement, equal rights and sex education?

Goal 4 is high-quality lifelong education for all – but there is no consensus on what we actually mean by this laudable ambition.

The world is changing rapidly. New technology is presenting new opportunities. Globalisation is placing new demands on society. If the UN 2030 Goals are to be achieved, and we are to achieve the type of future to which the nations of the world have stated that they aspire, children and young people will need the right skills to navigate this new reality.

Unfortunately, in many countries, issues like climate change, equality and democracy are simply not on the curriculum – resources are so limited that schools find it impossible to employ modern teaching methods, and don't have access to tools like computers, smartphones and the internet.

High-quality teachers are a prerequisite for high-quality education – as are settings conducive to concentration and learning. Lack of electricity makes some classrooms freezing cold or boiling hot. Lack of drinking water reduces the ability to focus. Schools are often not built for disabled people, and don't provide them with the help and support they need.

Improving education for all would lift huge numbers of people out of poverty. According to UNESCO, education increases earnings by roughly 10% per each additional year of schooling. It also estimates that youth education for all by 2030 would help to raise 60 million people out of poverty by 2050.

For this to happen would require a greater number of appropriately qualified teachers and better schools that change with the times. The goal of high-quality education for all is not just about academic and practical skills – it is also about values such as respect and understanding for others.

04. CREATE
OSCAR MURILLO

"THE WORLD IS SO MUCH MORE COLOURFUL, RESILIENT AND STRONG THAN SOME IN SOCIETY WOULD MAKE US BELIEVE"

Do you remember doodling at school? Phrases and slogans, or maybe the name of somebody you had a crush on, your football team, a sketch of your dog, or snatches of poetry. Nearly everybody does it.

School pupils have an urge to express themselves, and Colombian-born artist Oscar Murillo draws on this in *Frequencies*, a collaboration with thousands of children. He has placed canvases on desks in schools around the world and invites pupils to write and draw whatever pops into their heads.

The images that come back portray wildly different worlds. Love hearts and hashtags, guns and helicopters, a lone Christmas tree on a background of scribbles, flags, flowers, green mountains, phone numbers, police cars, peace signs... each of the 20,000+ canvases to date provides insight into the pupils' day-to-day lives and life in the classroom.

"The children's physical environment and the lives that they live vary greatly. That shows clearly," Murillo says.

Some canvases are full of colour, reflecting a world where the children have access to crayons and paints in the classroom, others are sprawling miniature worlds in hues of greys and blues, created mainly by pens and pencils. The lives of the children can be traced not only in doodles but in smears, stains, cuts, dust, patina, fingerprints ...

Even the children who may draw and write little still leave their marks as the canvases become part of the

OSCAR MURILLO

Born in Colombia, lives and works in various locations. His practice includes performance, installation, publishing, painting and sculpture. **Artwork:** *Frequencies*, 2013-.

classroom and gradually evolve into microcosms, taking on a life of their own and telling a tale of the differences and similarities.

In a way, the canvases can be compared with social media's streams of images and words.

"What is different here is simply that the children have a platform of fluid engagement, not mediated, allowing for conscious and unconscious engagement," explains Oscar Murillo.

"Children draw in a direct way. They want to discover the world, to get involved, to gather information, to grow – and all of that makes its way on to their desks, where many of them spend a large part of their day. For them, this expressiveness is absolutely natural," Murillo says.

04. THINK

WANTED: 69 MILLION NEW TEACHERS

SCHOOL TEACHERS ARE OFTEN UNDERPAID AND UNDERVALUED, BUT WE NEED TO FIND ANOTHER 69 MILLION OF THEM TO PROVIDE EDUCATION FOR ALL CHILDREN AND YOUNG PEOPLE. THE SHORTAGE OF TEACHERS THREATENS TO UNDERMINE PROGRESS ON EVERY ONE OF THE UN SUSTAINABLE DEVELOPMENT GOALS

Education is the key to a good life. It has a huge impact on our opportunities and social and technological advancement. It makes a difference to everything from income, health and housing, to gender equality, tolerance and participation in society. UN 2030 Goal 4 is about quality education for all – and only massive investment will make it happen.

Nine out of ten children now attend school – a massive leap forward compared to just a few years ago – but the quality of the education often leaves a great deal to be desired. In many countries, teachers are not respected or well paid. UN estimates suggest that almost 620 million children and young people – a staggering 60% – still lack basic reading and computing skills, even after years at school.

They include 263 million who have never set foot in a school, many but by no means all of whom are in sub-Saharan Africa. All over the world, it is always the poorest and most marginalised children who are either unable to attend school or have to make do with inadequate teaching by unqualified teachers. Education is a human right – but without qualified teachers, it is a right that doesn't amount to much.

The bad news is that qualified teachers are in such short supply that there is a real risk that the target of quality education for all will elude us. In fact, the UN estimates that it would take an additional 69 million trained teachers. The shortfall is particularly extreme at secondary level – 44.5 million according to the UN. Parts of Africa and Asia are also short of teachers at elementary level. Sub-Saharan Africa has the fastest-growing population of children and young people of school age, but 70% of countries in the region don't have enough teachers to provide even elementary schooling.

In some schools, shortages mean class sizes of 150+ and a lack of tables and chairs. The classrooms are frequently so hot that the children and teachers find it difficult to concentrate. Lots of children just give up, and many more only stick around until they finish their basic education.

Another problem is the lack of supply teachers. Schools often have to close when teachers are ill, a problem that is particularly rife in the poorest

Egyptian pupils during a lesson in a primary school near Giza. The classrooms are crowded, with up to 70 pupils per class. Often, there are not enough desks for all of them.

countries and areas, e.g. in Senegal, where they fail to open for an average of 50 out of the 188 school days. Shortages also mean that management often turns a blind eye when teachers are accused of sexually abusing or beating pupils. Some girls drop out when they reach puberty in order to avoid abuse by male teachers and pupils. Teachers simply aren't trained to deal with male pupils abusing their female classmates, so it often continues until the girls just leave.

Most teachers also lack skills in dealing with minority groups or vulnerable, ill or disabled children.

One of the big problems is that teachers are often both underpaid and undervalued. The best-qualified ones often prefer to work in private schools. In some countries, wages are linked to performance, so it is far more attractive to teach only the most promising students. Studies have shown that this exacerbates inequality, with the most vulnerable students often left with the worst teachers and least attention.

Another reason for shortages is that teaching is just not seen as an attractive job – and not only in developing countries. In the West, the large number of teachers who will retire over the next few years also poses a problem. Younger generations are enjoying greater career freedom than ever, and are unlikely to opt for a profession that heaps ever-increasing pressure on them while freezing their wages.

According to the United Nations Educational, Scientific and Cultural Organization (UNESCO), there is an urgent need for massive global investment in schools, especially in the training and recruitment of teachers. In many parts of the world, the trend is going in the opposite direction, and development aid for education has also stagnated.

Internet-based education and training is one way of reaching more people and upskilling teachers. It is already used in many parts of the world, including China, where it is often difficult to recruit and retain teachers in rural areas. Online classes have helped make school more attractive for both pupils and teachers. Pupils can learn about subjects despite shortages of qualified teachers in their local area, while teachers feel less isolated and have colleagues to use as sounding boards.

While this is a positive development, online solutions are not enough on their own. Good teachers do more than just convey knowledge – school is also the place where children and young people develop as individuals and learn to interact with and respect others. UNESCO is calling on the nations of the world to make teaching a more attractive profession and to invest in education for the most vulnerable and marginalised groups.

It is not just the progress toward UN 2030 Goal 4 that rests on the number of qualified teachers and education for all – falling short on number 4 jeopardises every single one of the 17 goals.

COOKERS – THE KEY TO EDUCATION?

What if girls spent an extra 102 hours on their education every year? Or women spent that amount of time on retraining and skills enhancement?

The public-private initiative Clean Cooking Alliance estimates that families using wood or coal-fired stoves spend an average of 102 hours a year collecting wood – many of them more – and it's usually women and girls who do it. Cooking like this takes time and it's a dirty business. Soot emissions also mean you have to keep cleaning the house and your clothes – time that would be better spent learning.

Poor families often think that gathering fuel and cooking are more important than their daughters' education. On average, women work 10–40% longer every day than men – and much of this is down to poor cooking facilities. The negative impact on job opportunities, earnings potential and education deprives them of the chance to improve their living standards.

According to the UN, about 40% of the world's population are dependent on wood, coal or other natural fuels for cooking – a dependency with serious side effects. Air pollution causes millions of deaths every year, half of which are due to inefficient stoves. Small children are particularly vulnerable. Deforestation caused by the demand for firewood also exacerbates climate change and destroys the natural habitats of an untold number of species. The solution is cleaner and more

On the island of Quelelene, Mozambique, women and girls are responsible for collecting firewood.

efficient cookers that use less fuel and free up time, including for education. There are plenty of alternative models, even for houses not on the electricity grid.

The biggest problem is money – but various options are being explored, including various types of micro-payment.

INTERNET CLASSROOMS

Millions of people all over the world educate themselves without ever setting foot in a classroom. Online platforms like Udemy, Coursera and Khan Academy provide everything from short courses in accountancy, drawing and programming to full bachelor and master's degrees.

Khan Academy is one of the oldest and best-known platforms. Salman Khan started using online software to teach his cousin maths in 2008. When other relatives asked for help too, he started posting short YouTube video lessons. Seeing the potential to make education accessible to all, he quit his job to focus on what would become Khan Academy. School pupils, students and teachers all over the world now use his platform in several languages. Video is still the main medium, but other online tools are also used.

Khan Academy is a free supplement to other forms of learning. It helps with homework and teaches extra skills. Platforms like Coursera provide everything

from short courses to full university-level degrees. Two professors from Stanford founded it in 2012 after they realised that online teaching could reach more students in a month than they would in their entire career by conventional means.

Online teaching by qualified teachers from accredited institutions is enormously beneficial to students in places where they don't have access to anything similar. It also help patients confined to their home or a hospital, and people with jobs who don't have the time or money to study full-time.

Studies have shown that online education is not only as effective as a conventional classroom – in some cases, it's even better – partly because online courses are often interactive and can be tailored to the needs of the individual. Another benefit is that thousands of virtual classmates are on hand to provide support and feedback – day and night.

The benefits are obvious, but the full potential of online learning will only be fully realised when internet access is universal and affordable. Until then, the poor will continue to struggle to obtain a good education – online or off.

04. ACT
I'LL GET MARRIED WHEN I WANT TO

CHILD MARRIAGE IS ONE OF THE BIGGEST BARRIERS TO EDUCATION THAT GIRLS FACE. MEMORY BANDA WAS 13 WHEN SHE CHANGED THE LAW IN MALAWI BY SAYING NO

Everybody thought Memory would follow in the footsteps of the vast majority of other young girls in her city in southern Malawi – i.e. she would be sent to what might euphemistically be called a "marriage preparation camp" and then married off. Half of all women in Malawi are married before the age of 18. Many of them are sent to sexual initiation camps, where girls as young as nine are forced to have sex with older men.

Memory has seen what this does to girls, among them her sister, who was sent away aged 11 and was soon pregnant – by no means an unusual fate in these camps. Many of the girls find themselves pregnant and are quickly married off, often to violent, dominating and significantly older husbands. They no longer go to school, lose all autonomy over their own lives, some contract HIV, others die due to the trauma of giving birth so young.

Memory said no to all of this. She got in touch with a local grassroots organisation that campaigned against child marriage, sparking what would become a lengthy battle to uphold the rights of girls and make their voices heard. She ran workshops that allowed girls and young women to share their opinions about child marriage. Eventually, local politicians listened and set a local age limit for marriage.

But Memory didn't stop there. She drummed up more and more support for her campaign. In 2015, the government set 18 as the national age limit for marriage. It was a major victory, but not the end of the matter for Memory. The legislation has had an impact on child marriages and the camps, but it did not shut them down completely. Another problem is that girls are still dropping out of school – not least because of abuse by teachers, who are almost always men, and by male fellow students.

"It's not enough just to end child marriage," she says.
"We need equal rights for women."

Memory Banda's fight against child brides was successful, but there is still a lot to be done, she says.

GOAL 05

- -

GENDER EQUALITY

- -

"GENDER EQUALITY IS ALSO A MEN'S ISSUE.

The more I have spoken about feminism the more I have realized that fighting for women's rights has too often become synonymous with man-hating. This has to stop! Men are also imprisoned by gender stereotypes, and gender equality is their issue too. When they are free, things will change for women as a natural consequence. Feminism is the belief that men and women should have equal rights and opportunities. It is the theory of the political, economic and social equality of the sexes. These rights I consider to be human rights"

MARTA VIEIRA DA SILVA

6 times FIFA World Player of the Year, UN Women Goodwill Ambassador

Previous double page: Cotton harvest near Banfora, Burkina Faso
(10° 48' N – 3° 56' W)

GOAL 05
ACHIEVE GENDER EQUALITY AND EMPOWER ALL WOMEN AND GIRLS

The vision: By 2030, all women and girls everywhere will no longer be subject to discrimination, violence and exploitation. Harmful practices such as early and forced marriage and female genital mutilation will be eliminated. Everyone will have access to sexual and reproductive health and rights. Women will have equal rights to economic resources, land, property and inheritance, and will occupy leadership roles at all levels of decision-making in political, economic and public life. New technology will be used to promote the empowerment of women

49
COUNTRIES HAVE
NO LEGISLATION ON
DOMESTIC
VIOLENCE

THE LAW
FAILS WOMEN

A NUMBER OF COUNTRIES
STILL HAVE NO
LEGISLATION PROTECTING
WOMEN FROM VIOLENCE
AND SEXUAL ABUSE

(**Source:** UN Women: Turning Promises into
Action: Gender Equality in the 2030 Agenda
for Sustainable Development, 2018)

45
COUNTRIES HAVE NO
LEGISLATION THAT
SPECIFICALLY ADDRESSES
SEXUAL
HARASSMENT

35%
OF ALL WOMEN HAVE
EXPERIENCED
SEXUAL
OR PHYSICAL
VIOLENCE

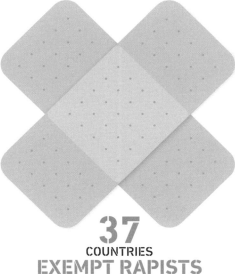

37
COUNTRIES
EXEMPT RAPISTS
FROM PROSECUTION
IF THEY ARE MARRIED TO
OR SUBSEQUENTLY MARRY
THE VICTIM

GREATER KNOWLEDGE,
GREATER EQUALITY

Women and girls still don't enjoy the same rights as their male counterparts in many spheres of life. They are discriminated against, harassed, sexually assaulted and paid less, they are under-represented in management and politics, risk being married against their will, and are often denied reproductive autonomy.

Nobody knows the real extent of gender inequality. The statistics we do have are often out of date, we lack information from large numbers of the poorest places in the world, and often about minorities as well. Many countries simply don't collate data on issues that would shed light on where gender inequality is at its worst, and whether the situation is improving or not.

Data is knowledge, and knowledge is power and the path to change. To guarantee equal rights, we need to know more about the situations in which women find themselves. But despite the huge volumes of data currently generated, large gaps remain in our knowledge about the living conditions faced by women and girls.

The majority of the 17 UN 2030 Goals are predicated on achieving gender equality – and the existing figures show that the position of women is significantly worse than that of men. At the moment, we have insufficient data for 80% of the indicators needed to provide a clear picture of the current situation and the direction in which it is heading. For a start, only 13% of the nations of the world budget for gender-based statistics.

The UN programme "Make Every Woman and Girl Count" encourages official agencies, companies, research institutions and civil society to work together to enhance knowledge and generate better data. Five years from now, we hope to have a far better overview of issues like the prevalence of gender-discriminatory legislation, how much women own and earn, the extent of violence against girls and women, the state of women's political representation, and how much unpaid work is performed by women and girls compared to men.

Although gathering data is no guarantee that targets will be met, it sheds light on issues, and it is easier to follow up on policy decisions if they are evidence-based

05. CREATE
JENNY HOLZER
"ROMANTIC LOVE WAS INVENTED TO MANIPULATE WOMEN"

"RAISE BOYS AND GIRLS THE SAME WAY"
The American conceptual artist Jenny Holzer has emblazoned her simple but powerful statements on T-shirts, on posters and in giant letters against a pink backdrop on an electronic sign in a stadium. It is typical of her bold approach over the last 40-plus years.

Words are her preferred art form, and her works pop up wherever they will have the greatest impact. She once mentioned in an interview that when her daughter was young, she thought that all electronic signs were by her mum. Not quite, perhaps, but Holzer has presented her own words and those of others at some hugely iconic locations – from Times Square in New York to the Reichstag in Berlin and Blenheim Palace near Oxford.

She transfers the techniques and aesthetics of advertising to benches, baseball caps, stickers and even condom wrappers, spreading words and sentences that are sometimes angry, occasionally disturbing, often poetic, affectionate, political or humorous.

The relationship between the sexes has occupied her throughout her career. Statements such as

"AFTER DARK IT'S A RELIEF TO SEE A GIRL WALKING TOWARD OR BEHIND YOU. THEN YOU'RE MUCH LESS LIKELY TO BE ASSAULTED" and "MEN DON'T PROTECT YOU ANYMORE" force us to stop and contemplate their validity.

We are bombarded with messages from all sides, which is precisely why it is valuable to be jolted out of a state of passive consumption and into one in which we actively consider these messages. Are they necessarily true simply because they're presented in a way that's bright and beautiful, or in gigantic fonts and capital letters?

Holzer still displays her works in various locations, only now she often uses other authors' words, amplifying their messages on buildings and electronic signs when she feels that they deserve a wider audience.

JENNY HOLZER

American neo-conceptual artist, based in New York. The main focus of her work is the delivery of words and ideas in public spaces. **Artworks:** *GOBO*, 2012. light projection. *Truisms: Raise boys and girls…*, 2015 (detail), marble footstool.

05. THINK
CLOSING THE DIGITAL GENDER GAP

DIGITAL TECHNOLOGIES CAN SUPPORT THE UN 2030 GOALS AND BRING PROSPERITY TO MORE PEOPLE. HOWEVER, MOST OF THE WORLD'S POOR, ESPECIALLY WOMEN, HAVE LITTLE OR NO ACCESS TO THEM

Whether it's a farmer checking the market price of milk, a company filing export papers or a consumer paying a bill, more and more of our everyday lives are conducted online, via a mobile phone or computer.

Digital technology solves all sorts of problems, but more often than not the main beneficiaries are men rather than women. The digital gender gap has exacerbated some of the discriminatory structures that already made it more difficult for women to earn as much as men and to exert the same degree of influence.

Research shows that the digital gender gap not only exists, but in some cases is getting wider by the year. For example, 10% fewer women than men have access to a mobile phone. The corresponding figure for mobile internet access is 26%. Men also use the internet more than women. The gap here is 12%, rising to 33% in the least developed countries.

All over the world, women are under-represented in information and communication jobs. The world's first digital computer, ENIAC, was programmed exclusively by women, but they have since been all but forced out of the industry. No reliable global figures are available, but in the US only around a quarter of technology jobs

are held by women – even though women account for 57% of all jobs in the country. In the developing world, the difference is even greater.

The gap is also huge when we look at the top jobs in the technology sector – in the EU, only about 10% are held by women. One unfortunate consequence of this is that many of the problems faced by women go unnoticed by the very people trying to solve them.

Technology isn't the only obstacle that women face. Globally, two out of every three illiterate people are women. On top of that, many women in the poorest parts of the world only speak the local language, which digital systems often don't support.

It is absolutely critical that women are given better access to technological solutions and jobs. Klaus Schwab, the founder of World Economic Forum, sees it as a question of justice as well as economics.

"Achieving gender equality is obviously necessary for economic reasons. Only economies that make full use of all their talent will remain competitive and prosper. But even more important, gender equality is a matter of justice. As a human race, we also have an obligation to promote a balanced set of values."

THE UNVALUED WORK OF WOMEN

When Leymah Gbowee, the Liberian recipient of the Nobel Peace Prize, spoke at the Bill & Melinda Gates Foundation's Goalkeepers conference in 2017, she shared an anecdote about a man she had met in a village. Women and feminism bugged him.

"All we hear about is women, women, women!" he snapped and complained that his wife just spent his money and gossiped.

Leymah asked the man how much he earned, and he told her. She then asked about all the things his wife did at home – dishes, cleaning, childcare. She noted it all down – every last task.

They then tallied up how much it would cost to pay to have it all done by somebody else. Had she been paid for it, the woman would have earned more than her husband. But her work was – quite literally – not valued.

In every country across the world, women still do the vast majority of housework and care duties – an estimated 75%. Women spend between one and three hours more per day on housework than men, according to UN Women, and up to ten times as long caring for children.

The work done by women may not show up in national accounts and budgets, but the UN estimates its accounts for up to 40% of GDP in some countries.

The unequal distribution of unpaid labour means that women are at greater risk of being poor. They frequently work part time or in subordinate roles and are grossly over-represented in sectors in which low wages are rife.

The amount of domestic work leaves less time for hobbies, political engagement or further training or education, which has significant consequences for the ability to exert influence on society.

A solution could be to acknowledge the valuable work that women do, distribute the workload more evenly and empower women at all levels of society.

EQUALITY AND POPULATION GROWTH

Gender equality does so much more than just improve the lives of individuals. It is the key to tackling climate change, sustainable use of resources, decent jobs, lower crime rates and better health for women and their families, to name but a few of the benefits.

The ever-rising population curve is often cited as a barrier to getting to grips with climate change, poverty and hunger. What is often overlooked is that the global fertility rate – the average number of births per woman – has dropped dramatically in recent decades as education has improved and women have fought for and won the right to choose.

According to the independent Brookings Institution in America, women with no education have an average

of four or five more children than those who complete their schooling. Half a century ago, women gave birth to an average of five children, a figure that has now dropped below 2.5 globally.

Despite this progress, the number of people on the planet is still rising – due mainly to longer life expectancy and more women reaching childbearing age. On a brighter note, this appears to be a transitional phase. The trend is projected to flatten out by 2100.

Education also increases the likelihood of women exerting greater control over their bodies and avoiding unwanted pregnancies.

The Drawdown project, which conducts research into climate solutions, mentions women's education and access to contraception and family planning as two of the most effective investments. Gender equality isn't just good for women – it's good for everyone.

05. ACT
HANNA NAIMA McCLOSKEY: ENCODING JUSTICE

Hanna McCloskey (top left) and attendees at the
Fearless Futures Summer Leadership Institute.

"IF WE WANT A FUTURE WITH EQUAL OPPORTUNITIES FOR ALL, WE HAVE TO BE AWARE OF THE OPPRESSION AND INJUSTICE BUILT INTO SOCIETY AT THE MOMENT"

HANNA McCLOSKEY, FOUNDER AND CEO OF FEARLESS FUTURES

McCloskey rejects the terms "bias" or "unconscious" when talking about inequity. She believes that the vast majority of people are not deliberately cruel or prejudiced, but that we need to be clear that profound injustice and oppression have been designed into our society.

"It is a state of affairs that we can and must change. It's not simply the way that things are. These are injustices built up over a long time, and we have a duty to be aware of them," says McCloskey.

Fearless Futures was born of her anger at the injustices that she saw in the financial world, where a glass ceiling remains stubbornly in place. But she was much younger when she first noticed the oppression of those who don't fit into a "male, pale, and stale" world dominated by white, middle-aged men.

"I grew up in Britain, and my mother, while British, is an Algerian Muslim migrant to the UK. It didn't take me long to realise that the mainstream narrative for the inequity women experience only spoke about it from a white, middle-class perspective. My mother didn't fit into that category, so her life and the challenges she faced simply weren't part of the debate," she adds.

McCloskey became interested in how injustices are designed into the system, whether it be gender, sexuality, disabilities, race, class, religion or other traits.

"A lot of patterns make some people more vulnerable than others – gender is just one of them. If you don't fit into all of the boxes that a tiny section of society has defined as the 'right' ones, then you stick out all the time. It becomes more difficult to be heard. You find that everything has been set up to suit other people," McCloskey explains.

The realities of gender inequality became all too real when McCloskey started work in a bank. Angered by the automatic assumptions about who could and couldn't do what, amongst other things, she quit to set up an organisation dedicated to making society more inclusive on all levels, and to challenging entrenched attitudes to gender and race.

The work done by Fearless Futures includes educational programmes for young people that raise awareness of the inequities that dominate society, their communities and themselves. "The programmes focus on challenging the narrow, prevailing notions of what constitutes masculinity, for example. The current model is very limiting for all genders," she says.

Fearless Futures also takes its message into workplaces, where it trains corporate leaders about designed inequalities, and critically examines the mechanisms and assumptions that make it easier for middle-class, white, cisgender, heterosexual, non-disabled men, for example, to succeed.

"To change these narrow and restrictive ideas, it's not enough to compensate for the symptoms of inequities. We need to eliminate the root causes," she adds.

McCloskey acknowledges that progress has been made and that equality is now much more on the agenda.

"But there are still huge differences between how much men and women earn, the jobs they get, etc. Also, the problem is that we focus on each injustice separately. Gender injustice in this box, racial injustice in that box, and so on. But they're all linked. They're underpinned by the same mechanisms. And some people exist across multiple injustices. If we want to get to grips with the roots of inequality, we have to accept that it's a complex issue," she says.

This complexity explains why Fearless Futures does not focus exclusively on gender, but on discrimination in the widest and deepest sense. The goal is not equality, but justice.

"When we speak about equality on its own, the goal often becomes introducing things like networks for specific groups. But when we speak about justice, we focus on removing the barriers that prevent some people from participating in society fully, in a way that ensures dignity, legitimacy, freedom, safety and belonging," says McCloskey.

One important element of the work of Fearless Futures is its efforts to literally encode justice into the future. New technology may offer huge opportunities, but even the most sophisticated applications and machines are only as smart as their coding – they are entirely dependent on the input they receive, which is based on existing and historical data. If technology is not coded in a way that allows it to recognise and remove injustices and discrimination, then it may reproduce or even reinforce them, McCloskey warns.

"Our historical sources, our datasets and the way in which we do things are based on certain views of the world. For example, black people are still far more likely to be stopped and searched by the police, because of the deeply entrenched and long-held racist idea that that they are dangerous. If we allow machines to uncritically absorb the details of existing material, they will perpetuate the same assumptions."

McCloskey cites the article by scholar Sascha Costanza Chock "Design Justice, AI and Escape from the Matrix of Domination" as an example of how body scanners in airports become sites of "sociotechnical reproduction of the gender binary" and where those who don't fall neatly into "man" or "woman", as may be the case for trans people, set off the alarm.

"The article speaks of the acute stress of approaching the milimeter wave scanning machine anticipating all that will follow if the alarm goes off as their body is 'flagged as anomalous'. Through this lens we see both how cis people's privilege and power moving through the world is designed, and how it must also be possible – and indeed urgently needed – to start from the design principle of encoding justice into technology."

CLEAN WATER AND SANITATION

"THE GLOBAL GOALS ARE A REMARKABLE ACHIEVEMENT, AGREED BY 193 NATIONS – A COMPLEX YET PRACTICAL ANALYSIS OF THE ISSUES FACING THE WORLD.

They are the only plan on the table for us to be the first generation to end extreme poverty, the last to be threatened by climate change, and the most determined to fight inequality and injustice. We need to fight harder than ever before to turn promises into reality – collectively we can achieve these 17 amazing goals and leave the greatest possible legacy to future generations. And I think creativity is going to be central to this - my motto is 'in order to make things happen, you have to make things.' And imagination and inspiration and originality are ALWAYS going to be crucial for campaigning to really catch fire"

RICHARD CURTIS
Writer, producer, founder of Project Everyone

Previous double page: Fisherman on the lake at the Imboulou Hydroelectric Dam on the river Lefini, Pool Region, Republic of the Congo (2° 56' 14.06" S – 16° 2' 6.93" E)

GOAL 06
ENSURE ACCESS TO WATER AND SANITATION FOR ALL

The vision: By 2030, all people will have equal access to safe and affordable drinking water. Everyone will have access to adequate sanitation and hygiene, and the practice of open defecation will be a thing of the past. In order to improve water quality, pollution will be reduced, dumping will be eliminated, and the emissions of hazardous materials will be minimised. The proportion of untreated wastewater will be halved. Improved water-resource management and more efficient water use will substantially reduce scarcity. Water-related ecosystems, such as mountains, forests, wetlands, rivers and lakes, will be restored and protected

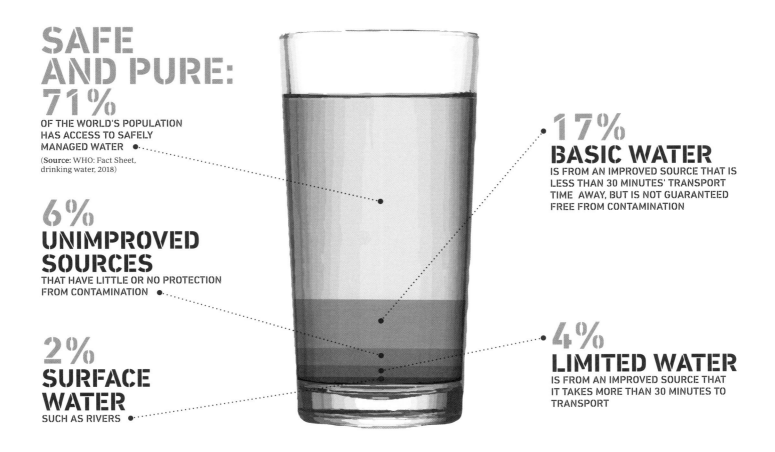

SAFE AND PURE: 71%
OF THE WORLD'S POPULATION HAS ACCESS TO SAFELY MANAGED WATER
(**Source:** WHO: Fact Sheet, drinking water, 2018)

17% BASIC WATER
IS FROM AN IMPROVED SOURCE THAT IS LESS THAN 30 MINUTES' TRANSPORT TIME AWAY, BUT IS NOT GUARANTEED FREE FROM CONTAMINATION

6% UNIMPROVED SOURCES
THAT HAVE LITTLE OR NO PROTECTION FROM CONTAMINATION

4% LIMITED WATER
IS FROM AN IMPROVED SOURCE THAT IT TAKES MORE THAN 30 MINUTES TO TRANSPORT

2% SURFACE WATER
SUCH AS RIVERS

WATER AND PEACE

Without food, humans can survive for weeks. Without water, only days. Clean drinking water is the planet's most precious resource, but water shortages are a huge problem in many parts of the world – and the situation is getting worse.

Sub-Saharan Africa and western Asia are the worst-affected areas, but technologically developed countries are by no means immune to droughts, which endanger humans and animals and destroy crops. If we continue to use water as we currently do, half of the world's population will live in water-stressed areas by 2025.

Billions of people are affected, directly and indirectly, by a lack of water. Clean water is essential for drinking and sanitation, and without it, the risk of infectious and potentially fatal diseases and epidemics is greatly multiplied. In many countries, the nearest source is often some distance away. The long walk to fetch water reduces the time families have available to earn a living. It also prevents many girls – whose job it is to collect the water – from attending school. To compound matters, it is often so expensive that water absorbs much of the family budget.

Access to clean water is also a critical factor in regional and national conflicts, as well as migration, as waves of migrants relocate in search of safe supplies for themselves and their livestock.

Agriculture is the biggest single user, with irrigation and livestock needs swallowing up 70% of the world's fresh water. Industry is also a major culprit, and many industrialised nations provide no meaningful incentives to curb excesses. Individual consumers bear some responsibility too – in some American suburbs, 80% of household water goes on gardens and swimming pools and watering a small lawn can take more than 1,000 litres.

If we are to achieve the global goal of clean drinking water for all – not to mention peace, security, health, sustainable consumption, economic growth, an end to hunger and the eradication of poverty – then we must decouple growth from water consumption. More growth must not mean more use of water.

We know it can be done. According to the United Nations Environment Program (UNEP), water use in Australia fell by 40% in the period 2001–2009 but the economy grew by more than 30%.

06. CREATE
YIN XIUZHEN

"AT THE MOMENT WE HAVE NOWHERE ELSE TO SURVIVE OTHER THAN
ON THIS PLANET, SO WE MUST RETHINK IN TERMS OF HOW TO COEXIST
WITH THIS LONELY PLANET"

Furniture coated in concrete dust; a comment on progress in China and on urban renewal in Beijing, where the clear blue sky of the past has in recent years been replaced by a never-ending smog. Rapid industrialisation may well have generated wealth and lifted millions out of poverty, but it is also the reason why Chinese parents – like Yin Xiuzhen herself – now strap facemasks to their children before they go to school.

Yin grew up during a period of huge upheaval in China. She witnessed the transition from Mao's cultural revolution, with its regimentation and collectivisation, to the prosperity of today, when the Chinese middle and upper classes are global consumers, and China helps set the international agenda.

The economic boom has been accompanied by a greater focus on the environment. Clean drinking water and air can no longer be taken for granted – no matter how abundant they once were. The extreme pollution of China's rivers and lakes gave Yin the idea for her *Washing the River* project back in the mid-1990s. Since then, she has applied the concept to other rivers around the world.

Yin takes water from the river and freezes it, forming large blocks of ice that the public then helps to cleanse. The pollution is unmistakable in a frozen block. She describes how it stirs something in the crowd – a profound urge to repair the damage already done.

YIN XIUZHEN

A leading female figure in Chinese contemporary art, notable for her early engagement with environmental concerns and the connection between memory and cultural identity.
Artworks: *Washing River*, 1995-. Next page: *Black Hole*, 2010-.

Her work *Black Hole* built from shipping containers resembles a cut diamond and invites contemplation on the longing for luxury and endless consumption.

Yin's art questions why we rush headlong into progress without really thinking about the consequences.

"As the environment deteriorates, it will no longer be able to provide mankind with the conditions for survival – so who are the results of this rapid development intended for?"

06. THINK
THE WATER WE EAT

"SAVE WATER, DRINK CHAMPAGNE!" WITTY SIGNS ARE TEN
A PENNY IN WINE BARS AND RESTAURANTS, BUT IN FACT,
IT TAKES SEVERAL LITRES OF WATER TO PRODUCE A SINGLE
GLASS OF THE GLORIOUS, BUBBLY STUFF

Not that champagne and wine are the biggest culprits in the world of food and drink. That dubious honour goes to beef. According to Water Footprint, it takes an average of a staggering 15,000+ litres of water to produce a kilogram of meat – mainly on the irrigation of feed crops but also water used to dilute waste from the production phase, during the slaughtering process and for the animals to drink. In terms of calories, it takes more than 10 litres of water to produce just one calorie of beef.

Beef may be an extreme case but cultivating food always uses water. Generally speaking, root vegetables tend to use the least, meat products the most. Specifically, vegetables, fruits and cereals are all better than meat; potatoes are better than rice; beer is better than wine, and pork and chicken are better than beef. Our choices can reduce consumption, but we can't avoid water altogether. Calculations of the volume used in food production suggest that we "eat" 3,500 litres of water a day. The UN estimates that 70% of fresh water is used for irrigation and livestock.

The project "The Water We Eat" shares a number of water-saving tips – and no, drinking champagne isn't one of them.

• **CUT DOWN ON MEAT**. It takes an extreme amount of water to produce a steak, which is one reason why vegetarians are responsible for half as much water consumption as meat-eaters. Even one meat-free day a week makes a difference, particularly in countries with a meat-heavy diet.

• **CHOOSE MEAT FROM ANIMALS RAISED ON GRASS.** A significant proportion of the water used in meat production is for animal fodder. Animals that graze in areas that don't require irrigation consume significantly less water than those reared in stalls.

• **AVOID FOOD WASTE.** When you throw out food, you effectively waste large amounts of good drinking water. With water scarce and under increasing pressure, and with 30% of the human race without access to clean water, that's just unethical.

EFFECTIVE IRRIGATION ISN'T ENOUGH ON ITS OWN

Traditional methods of watering crops mean that the plants don't absorb all of the water, so governments, farmers and agricultural organisations have joined forces to develop more efficient irrigation methods.

While this is undoubtedly good news for farmers, who'll be able to grow more and healthier crops with the same amount of water, it might not be such good news for their neighbours or the wider community, who are also reliant on water. Studies have revealed what experts have dubbed the "paradox of irrigation efficiency" – more efficient irrigation systems do not necessarily make more water available.

According to an article in *Science* in 2018, with traditional irrigation methods crops absorb around

40–70% of the water, 10–25% evaporates, and 15–50% seeps back into the local watershed. The exact percentages depend on variables like crops, soil and weather but a significant quantity always flows back into the local watershed, so whatever the farmers might think, it's not wasted. More efficient systems – e.g. drip irrigation just below ground level – mean that max. 10% of water returns to the watershed, and less water is available to others.

Another unintended consequence of greater efficiency is that farmers are either growing more crops using the same amount of water as before – or, in some cases, switching to more water-intensive crops.

The experts behind the *Science* article emphasise that all of the evidence suggests that efficient irrigation alone isn't sufficient to guarantee adequate water supplies for all. We have to assess the overall supply situation, analyse the water cycle, and if necessary place appropriate limits on the amounts used by individual farmers.

FLUSH-FREE TOILETS

Every day, all across the world, 60 billion litres of clean water are quite literally flushed down the pan. Modern toilets use far less water than older models, but even the most efficient new ones use several litres per flush. And eight times out of ten, it's just to flush away urine.

What if we didn't need to flush every time?

A range of solutions is now emerging to limit or eliminate the need to flush every time nature calls. One of them is a toilet that works without water, turning bodily waste into compost to be used as fertiliser. Unlike old-fashioned latrines, these modern models can be installed in houses or offices, and are used in exactly the same way as a normal toilet – the only difference is that there's no flush. The composting takes place in a closed system. As long as they are properly maintained, the toilets have no particular odour or hygiene issues.

One major advantage of this type of toilet is that they work in places without a mains water supply or water-treatment facilities, removing the risk of urine and faeces leaking into the soil.

A Brazilian inventor has come up with a different approach. He decided to fast until he came up with a good idea. On day four, he started thinking about whether we actually need to flush after each visit – and Piipee was born.

Piipee is a liquid that neutralises the smell and colour of urine. Touch-activated containers are installed in the toilets. Instead of flushing, users spray a small amount of the biodegradable and non-toxic substance into the pan.

The product is still being tested, but initial feedback, including from a big restaurant in Brazil, suggests it could cut water consumption – and bills – by more than half. The company behind Piipee estimates that cutting out flushing after urinating would reduce water consumption in households and companies by up to 80%.

06. ACT
JACK SIM:
POTTY TRAINING
THE WORLD

Jack Sim, also known as Mr. Toilet, has broken the taboo of "the Brown Agenda" as he calls it. In 2013, the UN General Assembly unanimously adopted World Toilet Organisation's founding day, 19 Nov, as the official UN World Toilet Day.

"I FOUND OUT THAT IT WAS ALMOST IMPOSSIBLE TO FIND A WAY TO TALK ABOUT HOW IMPORTANT IT IS THAT PEOPLE HAVE DECENT TOILET FACILITIES"

JACK SIM, FOUNDER OF THE WORLD TOILET ORGANIZATION

If you invert 007, you (kind of) get "LOO", a British colloquialism for "toilet". And what could be cooler than being the James Bond of sanitation? This is exactly the role played by former businessman Jack Sim, who has endowed the term "Royal Flush" with a whole new meaning and replaced the Walther PPK gun with a toilet plunger on a poster to promote "World Toilet Day", his own brainchild, which is held on 19 November and is now an official UN day.

Toilet humour is Sim's stock in trade and his most effective weapon in putting sanitation on the international political agenda.

"I found out that it was almost impossible to find a way to talk about how important it is that people have decent toilet facilities. Six out of ten people globally don't have access to safe sanitation, and that's a huge problem. It means diseases spread more easily and epidemics are more frequent," explains Mr Toilet, as he likes to call himself.

"But even though getting rid of what we have eaten and drunk is the most natural thing in the world, it's shrouded in taboo. We just don't talk about it. It's embarrassing, so it's not on the agenda, and we only talk about clean water. Humour puts sanitation on the agenda as an independent item. It breaks the taboo and does away with the embarrassment. When people laugh, they start to listen, and that's why I've adopted a humorous approach," he says.

Not that the consequences of so many people living without sanitation are any laughing matter. Every day, 1,000 small children die as a result of diarrhoea, deaths that better sanitation and clean water could have prevented.

"But there are other problems too. For example, in some parts of the world, the lack of cubicles with doors means that many women avoid drinking too much during the day so they can hold it in and don't have to risk exposing themselves in public. In some areas, venturing out at night also leaves women at risk of attack and abuse. Lack of safe sanitation has all sorts of consequences."

Globally, almost 900 million people still relieve themselves in fields, woods, or down back alleys because they just don't have a toilet. Three billion live in areas where human waste isn't treated or disposed of properly, or where several families share a single toilet – which also leads to a higher risk of disease.

In one sense, it was just by chance that Sim became involved in the sanitation issue. At 40, he was a highly successful businessman, independently wealthy after a career in the construction industry and didn't need to make any more money.

"I took stock of my life. I could have kept on working, but to what end? To earn even more money I didn't need? As a businessman, I knew that investing time in something useless was a bad deal, and it dawned on me that, if I kept working, I'd miss the opportunity to make a difference and help other people."

"Even then, it took a while before I found the right cause. A lot of causes already have great advocates. Businesses, politicians and NGOs are only too happy to back the blue and green agendas. But what about the brown one? It had been hidden and forgotten. I realised that something that we do six to eight times a day is part of our culture and important. So I adopted toilets as my cause," îsays Sim.

In 2001, he founded the World Toilet Organization, which is committed to improving sanitary conditions worldwide. It isn't always easy: "We made some beginners' mistakes. For example, we built toilets for a school in China. It was a beautiful building, and we patted each other on the back and congratulated ourselves on a job well done when we handed them over to the school. But when we came back a year later to see how they were getting on, we found that the headmaster had turned the toilets into his office because it was a far nicer building than the actual school," he laughs.

A follow-up visit to another site a year after its handover threw up a different but related anecdote.

"We were pleased to see how well they had cared for the building. The toilets were sparkling clean, and everything was like new. We praised them for taking such good care of it. 'Yes, it is so beautiful that we only use it for guests,' they explained. This, of course, wasn't what we intended, and we soon came to realise the importance of adapting new facilities to what already exists around them."

Sim and his organisation have made other discoveries along the way, including the need to work closely with the people you want to help and always be aware that their wants and needs may not be what you expect.

"You can't just impose solutions on people. Imagine a husband buying his wife a red dress when she hates the colour. Not everybody wants a toilet. It's easier to do what you've always done and pop out to the woods, rather than have to keep a new building clean. It takes dialogue to convince people of the benefits of a toilet. We also have to recognise the important social function, for many women in certain parts of the world, of getting together to go and do their business. It's a time and a place where they can be themselves, talk about their husbands and mothers-in-law, and enjoy a degree of freedom. A toilet at home would take all that away, so we have to find other solutions," says Sim.

Although it is sometimes difficult to get a hearing on toilet-related issues, Sim is an eternal optimist and notes increasing interest in, and understanding of, the importance of sanitation. He is also glad he decided to invest his energy in "the brown agenda", as he calls it.

"Time is the most important currency in life, not money. We need a new definition of wealth – in reality, we don't really need much in material terms. The definition of a millionaire should be somebody who helps a million other people."

AFFORDABLE AND CLEAN ENERGY

"LET'S SPEAK THE LANGUAGE OF THE PEOPLE WE WANT TO CONVINCE.

We need to embrace renewable energies and clean technologies because they are logical rather than just ecological. They create jobs and generate profit, while also reducing CO_2 emissions, improving health and preserving natural resources. Even if climate change didn't exist, they would make sense, as they represent the biggest industrial market of the century"

BERTRAND PICCARD

Initiator and Chairman of the Solar Impulse Foundation,
UNEP Goodwill Ambassador

Previous double page: Solar power plant in Sanlúcar la Mayor, near Seville, Andalusia, Spain
(37° 26' N – 6° 15' W)

GOAL 07
ENSURE ACCESS TO AFFORDABLE, RELIABLE, SUSTAINABLE AND MODERN ENERGY

The vision: By 2030, all people will have access to affordable, reliable and modern energy services. The share of renewable energy in the global energy mix will have increased substantially. Energy efficiency will not only have doubled, but will still be improving rapidly. There will be global co-operation aimed at facilitating access to clean energy research and technology. The developing and least developed countries, as well as small-island developing states, will have better infrastructure and technology in order to ensure modern, sustainable energy services

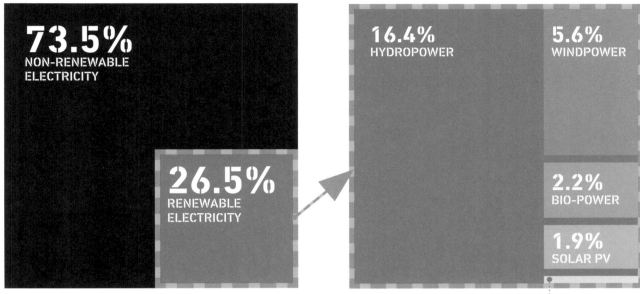

73.5%
NON-RENEWABLE
ELECTRICITY

26.5%
RENEWABLE
ELECTRICITY

16.4%
HYDROPOWER

5.6%
WINDPOWER

2.2%
BIO-POWER

1.9%
SOLAR PV

0.4%
OTHER
RENEWABLE
ENERGY
(E.G. OCEAN,
GEOTHERMAL)

POWERFUL RENEWABLES
**2017: RENEWABLES MAKE UP AN ESTIMATED
26.5 PERCENT OF THE GLOBAL ELECTRICITY PRODUCTION**
(**Source:** Renewables Global Status Report, 2018)

MY HOME, MY POWER PLANT

More than one billion people have no electricity, many of them because they live in places where it is difficult, expensive or impossible to connect to a grid. They are unable to do things others take for granted, which has a huge impact on their lives.

Without electricity, mundane tasks take far longer, eating up time that could be spent earning a living, going to school or doing homework. No electricity means no light by which to work, no access to news media, and no way of charging a mobile phone. It means food can't be refrigerated, which leads to costly waste and poses serious health risks.

On a larger scale, lack of power and unreliable supplies pose a danger to operations in hospitals and make it difficult to work or study in rooms that are too hot or too cold. Dreams of starting a business are often dashed because it is impossible to run them properly unless supplies are guaranteed.

Energy for all is a goal in itself, but it is also one of the UN 2030 Goals that has the greatest impact on the others – poverty, inequality, sustainability, climate, safe cities, decent working conditions, health and life on land.

The good news is that recent years have seen the emergence of new ways of generating electricity without the need for big, expensive power plants. Renewable energy sources like wind and solar power are becoming more affordable, and the infrastructure (e.g. solar cells and solar heaters) is taking up less and less physical space.

We now have the capacity to turn homes into self-sufficient miniature power plants. Small wind turbines, various forms of solar energy, biomass and local micro-networks will all help us reach the goal of clean energy for all by 2030.

But having the capacity is one thing – making use of it is another. In many countries, legislation, lack of funding and local payment models prevent these opportunities from being fully exploited. In other words, ensuring that everyone has access to electricity will require more than just new technology.

07. CREATE
JOHN GERRARD

"THE ONLY REASON WE DO NOT REALISE HOW FILTHY THE WORLD IS BECOMING IS BECAUSE OUR GREAT WASTE MATERIAL IS INVISIBLE. CARBON DIOXIDE HAS NO COLOUR, TASTE, OR SMELL"

What does power look like? If you were to create a portrait of power, what would you show?

For Irish artist John Gerrard, the answer is energy – specifically, the fossil fuels that underpin Western society as we know it. The word "power" has multiple meanings – authority, strength, energy – and it's no coincidence. "Much of what we think of as 'real' is a petroleum reality. Heat, comfort, mobility, it all comes from petroleum," he says.

Over the years, Gerrard has come to view our society as a sort of virtual oil state. It creates prosperity, but it is also extremely toxic. The downside to our insatiable appetite for oil is that it is fatal to all other life forms. The very same fossil fuel that ushered in the modern age and helped us expand across most of the planet has also exhausted huge landmasses and wiped out species at a rate unprecedented without a meteor strike or some other cataclysm of that magnitude.

Much of Gerrard's work revolves around our use of energy and the price that we – but especially the rest of the planet – pay for it. In *Smoke Tree* from 2006, a computer simulation shows smoking trees emitting CO_2 instead of oxygen. They are at once enchantingly beautiful and unsettling, endlessly moving sculptures in a bleak and deserted landscape.

The smoking trees, like many of Gerrard's other works, may look real, but they are virtual sculptures. His works

JOHN GERRARD

Irish artist, known for his sculptures, which typically take the form of digital simulations displayed using real-time computer graphics. **Artwork:** *Solar Reserve*, 2014.

simulate reality in real time – there's no footage to save and play back, and no two images look the same. The trees in the landscapes follow circadian rhythms and the passage of the seasons. They exist in a state of constant change. A couple of hundred years from now, the work will show a dying tree, slowly decaying.

Gerrard used the same technique in *Solar Reserve* in 2014, in which a computer simulation based on thousands of photos allows the viewer to observe a huge solar power plant in Tonopah, Nevada, where 10,000 panels convert sunlight into energy. The work meticulously simulates the movements of the Sun, Moon and stars as they appear in real time. Solar power may well be the energy of the future, but energy will still mean power.

07. THINK
FREE ENERGY FOR ALL?

COULD FUTURE ENERGY BE UNLIMITED, CHEAP AND CLEAN? A NUMBER OF NEW SOLUTIONS TO OLD DREAMS ARE ON THE HORIZON

Airborne wind turbines, solar farms in outer space, smart grids, fusion energy, wave power, volcanoes as heat sources... All over the world, experiments with alternative energy sources seek to replace the fossil fuels that have polluted our planet and triggered climate change. Experts think that we will only meet the energy needs of the future if we use a range of sources and solutions tailored to different needs and circumstances – from giant power plants to small-scale installations for individual households.

01. SOLAR ENERGY FROM OUTER SPACE

Every hour, the Sun sends more energy to the Earth than we need for a whole year. The process of harnessing solar power has come a long way since the first functional solar cell was developed in 1954. Solar energy has an increasingly large market share, and the technology is becoming more efficient all of the time.

The Sun, like wind, can supply energy to off-grid sites, which is good for people in remote areas. Nowadays, solar panels can be used as underlayers that produce energy and installed above water reservoirs, both to prevent evaporation during dry periods and to generate power.

However, until we learn to store energy better, solar power will be weather-dependent. And more than half of the energy from the Sun is lost on its way through the Earth's atmosphere. Placing solar farms in space, away from terrestrial weather systems, would guarantee solar power as long the panels remain on the day side of the Earth.

The idea of giant solar farms in space is nothing new. The technical challenges have proved insurmountable to date, but research continues apace. As space travel, wireless communication and solar power continue to mature, orbital solar farms come ever closer to reality. The Japan Aerospace Exploration Agency is conducting research into the concept, but it is by no means simple.

The plan is to use laser beams or microwaves to transfer the energy back to power plants. Small-scale experiments have already succeeded in doing so, and scientists predict that orbital solar farms could be a reality in 25 years.

02. AIRBORNE WIND TURBINES

Wind power may be a competitive and efficient means of producing energy – for example, it provided 43% of electricity in the record year of 2017 in Denmark – but it is not without its problems. The site has to be suitable, and potential neighbours often adopt a "not in my backyard" attitude. On the other hand, the

02. In an effort to harness strong, high-altitude wind, the company Altaeros has developed this cross between a traditional windmill and a blimp, called an aerostat.

03. Red-hot lava from the Bardabunga Volcano in Iceland. The nation has a long tradition of utilising geothermal energy.

winds are faster and more stable at higher altitudes, and experiments are being conducted with light, airborne turbines soaring like giant dragons up to 600 metres from the ground.

The long-term dream is to tap into the high-speed jet streams that continuously circle the planet, but developers say that the current crop of airborne wind turbines is already capable of producing twice as much energy as windmills on land.

03. HEAT FROM THE BOWELS OF THE EARTH

Countries with volcanic activity use geothermal power to heat buildings and water. Iceland has long been at the forefront of this technology. The Iceland Deep Drilling Project is now conducting experiments designed to take it to the next level, involving drilling five kilometres down, almost to the magma chambers, where the temperature is 4–500° Celsius. The idea is to pump water into a reservoir just above the magma, generating extremely hot steam to power turbines. Although this technology is still in its infancy, the energy company Statoil has invested in the Icelandic project and is confident of success.

04. FUSION ENERGY – THE SUCCESSOR TO TRADITIONAL NUCLEAR POWER?

When the first nuclear power plants were built in the 1950s, it was hoped that the technology would provide free and clean energy for all. These hopes were soon dashed as it became clear that they were expensive to build and maintain as well as inefficient in sparsely populated and remote areas. Radioactive waste also turned out to be a major problem, and the disasters at Chernobyl and Fukushima fuelled popular opposition. Traditional nuclear power is generated by fission. A neutron splits a heavy uranium nucleus, creating a chain reaction of further splits. Energy is released when a heavy core splits into lighter ones.

Fusion, by contrast, involves many light nuclei merging to form one large core. The same process takes place constantly in the Sun, which converts hydrogen into helium. It takes a great deal of energy, but releases far more. The main advantage over traditional nuclear power is that no radioactive material is required. The challenge is to generate temperatures high enough to ensure a stable fusion process for use in a power plant. Experiments have

04. A so-called BOLT Lifesaver from Fred Olsen Ltd at a US Navy demonstration site outside Hawaii.

been going on for decades, with some scientists joking that "fusion power is 30 years in the future – and always will be." Nevertheless, hopes remain high for this form of energy. If successfully harnessed, it will fulfil all the original promise of traditional nuclear power.

05. WAVE POWER

When the wind blows over the oceans, waves are formed, and they contain enormous amounts of energy. It is estimated that the waves along the west coast of America alone are equivalent to two-thirds of electricity demand in the entire USA.

Several countries already use wave energy in different ways, and various new types of technology are being developed, some of which will sit just below sea level, others along coasts.

In theory, wave power boasts a number of advantages, including that it is more predictable than wind power – wave patterns can be plotted up to 72 hours in advance, and the information factored into energy grids. Visually, wave farms are not as intrusive as large offshore wind farms either.

In practice, the situation is more complicated. The first wave-powered farm opened in Portugal in 2008 but had to close after just a few months due to technical problems. Other facilities have been damaged by storms or turned out not to be financially viable. Technology evolves all of the time, however, and the newest wave-capture systems are more robust and efficient than previous models, which has renewed faith in wave power as a future energy source.

06. SMART GRIDS

Smart grids have been around for a long time but are continually improving and becoming more efficient. They combine multiple energy sources and use big data to adapt supply and meet demand at all times and in the most efficient possible manner. More and more households have their own energy source – solar panels or small wind turbines – and any surplus is fed into the grid. Some of the latest smart grids can also link and include household boilers, heating them with surplus electricity so that they act as a form of energy store. And the grids can link batteries such as the ones used in electric cars and utilise them as storage capacity, as well as sending surplus energy from them back to the grid.

07. ACT
AN ENERGY REVOLUTION, ONE COMMUNITY AT A TIME

WHEN ENERGY PRICES PUSHED HER OWN COMMUNITY TO THE BRINK OF FINANCIAL RUIN, **DEANDREA SALVADOR** RESOLVED TO DO SOMETHING ABOUT THE SITUATION AND SET UP THE RENEWABLE ENERGY TRANSITION INITIATIVE (RETI) WHEN SHE WAS JUST 22

The climate in North Carolina ranges from scorching hot summers to bitterly cold winters, and people from the small community where DeAndrea Salvador was brought up weren't always able to afford comfortable temperatures. Families had to choose between food, medicine and energy.

While many Americans take for granted their heating, air-conditioning and other energy-guzzling appliances, poorer people struggle to pay their energy bills. In Salvador's community, the consequences were all too apparent. Illness was rife, and many were left feeling helpless as energy bills swallowed 20–30% of already meagre incomes.

Salvador wanted to do something about the problem. Since she was a teenager, she has worked with disadvantaged communities to raise awareness of energy efficiency and renewables, including by holding advice sessions and workshops.
"Sometimes, it doesn't take much. We've helped families cut their energy bills from $4–500 a month to $1–200. Simple things like covering windows with plastic in winter and insulating boilers make a big difference. Just showing people that solutions exist is one of our most important activities," she explains.

Salvador is also trying to drive the transition to renewables, one community at a time.

"I believe in working with small communities. They have so much to give," Salvador says. RETI's activities include setting up communal solar power units, crowdfunding and partnerships that allow the most impoverished communities to be part of the transition to renewables.

DeAndrea Salvador at the Charlotte Knights Stadium, speaking to middle schoolchildren about energy and sustainability.

DECENT WORK AND ECONOMIC GROWTH

"**TO DELIVER ON OUR PROMISE TO MAKE THE SUSTAINABLE DEVELOPMENT GOALS A REALITY FOR ALL, WE NEED EVERYONE** – and I mean everyone – to work together. We need investment bankers to work with rural farmers. Policy makers to strategise with activists. Young leaders to work with civil engineers. We need to invest in local economies so that resources are allocated in a way that overcomes exclusion and inequalities. We need to empower households, small businesses and local governments, ensure that people can get the finance they need to build better and more resilient futures"

ACHIM STEINER

Administrator, United Nations Development Programme

Previous Double Page: Mbeubeuss landfill in the Malika district of Dakar, Senegal
(14° 48' N – 17° 19' W)

GOAL 08
PROMOTE INCLUSIVE AND SUSTAINABLE ECONOMIC GROWTH, EMPLOYMENT AND DECENT JOBS FOR ALL

The vision: By 2030, economic growth will have continued, especially in developing countries. Global resource efficiency in production and consumption will have decoupled economic growth from environmental degradation. Women and men, regardless of age or disability, will have good jobs and receive equal pay for work of equal value. Young people will be in employment, education or training. Forced labour and the worst forms of child labour will be eradicated. Labour rights and safe and secure working environments for all, including migrant workers, will be protected and promoted

YOUTH UNEMPLOYMENT
GLOBALLY, 13.2 % OF PEOPLE BETWEEN 15 AND 24 ARE UNEMPLOYED
(**Source:** World Bank: Youth Unemployment, 2018)

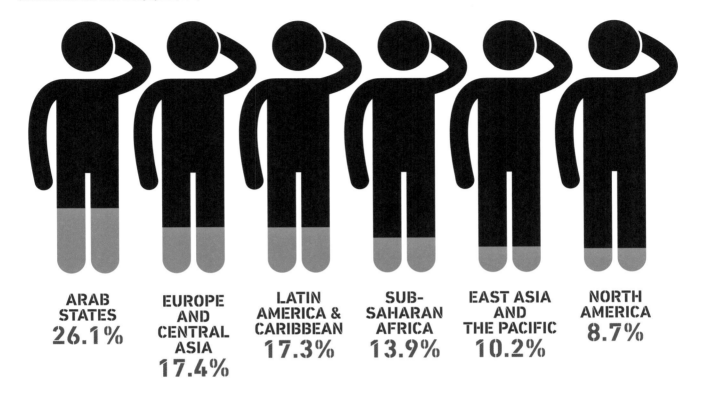

ARAB STATES
26.1%

EUROPE AND CENTRAL ASIA
17.4%

LATIN AMERICA & CARIBBEAN
17.3%

SUB-SAHARAN AFRICA
13.9%

EAST ASIA AND THE PACIFIC
10.2%

NORTH AMERICA
8.7%

A GENERATION IN LIMBO

To young people, a job is far more than just a way of earning money. It is a rite of passage. It is about standing on your own two feet. In some cultures, you are only considered an adult when you are financially independent. In others, it is when you marry or move into a home of your own. All of these things require money – and for most of us, that means having a job.

The UN estimates that around 71 million men and women aged 15–24 are unemployed. The true figure is likely to be even higher. Other studies suggest that nearly a quarter of a billion young people do not have a job. Others are on such low wages that they can't support a home and family. Many people work in the black economy, either at home or illegally abroad, rendering them vulnerable to exploitation. Some endure slave-like conditions, with few or no rights. Rampant youth employment is also a factor in crime and social unrest.

Global unemployment has risen in recent years. According to the UN, at least 470 million jobs will be required by 2030 just to satisfy the needs of new entrants to the labour market. The booming tourist industry offers some hope and is expected to create up to 90 million jobs in the next decade.

Another method of curbing youth unemployment is to provide more opportunities for young people to continue their studies, instead of leaving school as soon as possible. The inexorable rise of digitisation, automation and robots places new demands on recruits and their skills. Technological innovation still creates more jobs than it replaces, but these are often highly specialised. Education is the key to better pay, more opportunities and job security in times of crisis.

Young people are not the only ones affected by the lack of jobs – the challenge is to provide decent work for all. Technology can be a force for good. It could afford new opportunities to some of the most vulnerable groups in society, but that will require a concerted effort by all concerned.

08. CREATE
ALFREDO JAAR

"ARTISTS CREATE MODELS OF THINKING THE WORLD"

When gold was struck, more than 80,000 people, mainly men, were enticed away from their homes and families to the Serra Pelada mine in north-east Brazil. Its name, "the naked mountain", reflects the fact that the area was stripped of vegetation to extract the precious metal. It resembled a human anthill, crawling with thousands of people trying to make a life for themselves and enough money to support their families.

Serra Pelada is just a village now, and the opencast mine a polluted, poisonous lake. But the photos taken by Chilean artist Alfredo Jaar in 1985 could just as easily be from any number of mines now in any number of countries, where people still brave perilous conditions just to earn money. While undoubtedly dangerous, mines offer hope and an alternative to a grim future – they give people a chance to cheat the hand of fate. Health and safety and fair wages are still sacrificed to fuel the prosperity of others. The pictures of Serra Pelada remind us just how many people suffer to generate wealth from which they derive no benefit.

Jaar, a trained architect, has lived most of his life in the USA. His photos, films and installations tirelessly bear witness to the worst sides of human nature. He is perhaps best known for his documentation of the 1994 Rwandan genocide when close to a million people were exterminated in less than 100 days, in the face of the criminal indifference of the so-called "world community". His efforts were in vain, no one intervened, and the slaughter continued.

ALFREDO JAAR

Chilean-born artist, architect, and filmmaker. He is mostly known as an installation artist, often incorporating photography and covering socio-political issues and war. **Artworks:** *I Can't Go On. I'll Go On*, 2016. Next page: From the series *Gold In The Morning*, 1985.

Jaar himself has described his work as 99% thinking, 1% making.

"I do not create my works in the studio. I wouldn't know what to do. I do not stare at a blank page of paper and start inventing a world coming only from my imagination. Every work is a response to a real-life event, a real-life situation. Context is everything. My modus operandi has always been the same: before acting in the world, I need to understand the world."

I CAN'T GO ON
I'LL GO ON

08. THINK TOURISM IS GOOD, BUT NOT AT ANY COST

TRAVEL AND TOURISM ACCOUNTS FOR ONE IN TEN JOBS WORLDWIDE, GENERATES MORE THAN 10% OF GLOBAL REVENUE AND ACTS AS A CATALYST FOR GROWTH IN PERIPHERAL AREAS, FAR FROM THE URBAN HUBS. BUT TO MAKE THIS GROWTH SUSTAINABLE, TOURISM NEEDS TO BE PLANNED PROPERLY

Graffiti telling tourists to "piss off", eggs lobbed at sightseeing buses, demonstrations against cruise liners, crackdowns on services like Airbnb, banning tourists from local street markets, clampdowns on travel trollies... There is a yawning chasm between how tourism is viewed in many (especially European) cities, and the view of the UN World Tourist Organisation (UNWTO), which sees it both as a force for economic and social good and as a positive thing for nature and indigenous culture.

For UNWTO, tourism affords humanity one of the best opportunities to achieve a number of the UN 2030 Goals, with particular potential in areas ranging from poverty, women's rights, peace and tolerance, to quality, jobs and economic growth.

Tourism is already one of the biggest economic activities. In 2017, more than 1.3 billion people travelled abroad. UNWTO expects that figure to increase as more people are lifted out of poverty and have the opportunity to travel. In most countries, domestic tourism is also on the rise.

The industry accounts for one in ten jobs worldwide, providing employment for many people with no formal qualifications, often in the kind of far-flung places tourists want to visit where other employment opportunities are thin on the ground. Tourism is also one of the world's biggest exports – only fuel and chemicals are worth more.

Although tourism has the potential to make a positive impact in other areas, UNWTO warns that success should never be taken for granted, despite all the effort put into attracting tourism by many countries and regions. For it to be sustainable and positive, tourism needs to be planned and regulated, and the people affected by it need to be involved in the process. Otherwise, the opposite happens – as seen in places that have tipped over from mass tourism into overtourism.

The Dahshur pyramids in Egypt are a prime example of the positive impact of planned tourism. A UNESCO World Heritage Site, Dahshur is home to two of the best-preserved pyramids.

Venice is one of the world's most iconic and popular cities, but the crowds and huge cruise ships are threatening to ruin the attraction.

The Egyptian government and its UN partners were dogged in their pursuit of a plan that would preserve and protect the site but also bring social and economic benefits to the roughly 70,000 local people.

According to UNWTO, the project has created more than 500 permanent jobs and 350 seasonal ones so far – and the figures are set to rise as large numbers of tourists continue to flock to the pyramids. NGOs have helped locals source funding for small businesses and craft products, which are sold on site and exported. Some locals have also trained as guides. The community is involved in determining how tourism should develop in their area. Environmental improvements have already been made, as part of the project focuses on responsible waste management and another on special measures to protect biodiversity. Some local people have received specialised training in taking care of archaeologically valuable sites and objects. Women, in particular, have been able to earn more and make the most of new opportunities to start their own businesses.

According to UNWTO, listening to the wishes and expectations of local residents and involving them in decision making have been two of the most important aspects behind this success – more important than expanding tourist facilities. Ultimately, if the local people aren't on board, all the rest of it won't guarantee good results.

WHY TOURISM IS SO IMPORTANT

UNWTO's five pillars, where tourism can make a difference (UN World Tourist Organisation)

PILLAR 1: SUSTAINABLE ECONOMIC GROWTH

Tourism can create jobs and drive the establishment of new and innovative companies, making a positive impact on a range of other sectors, e.g. food production, entertainment, hotels and transport. However, all of this requires better management of the rapid growth in tourism, and that calls for investment, education and technology. It is also important to ensure that the local economy is resilient and won't collapse if visitor numbers fall.

PILLAR 2: SOCIAL INCLUSIVENESS, EMPLOYMENT AND POVERTY REDUCTION

The tourism industry depends on large numbers of people, making it an ideal sector for demographic groups who usually struggle to gain a foothold in the labour market – e.g. young people, women and the low-skilled. However, it is important that roles are clearly delineated, that there are opportunities for further training and that all jobs offer good working conditions. Tourism companies should also be encouraged to buy locally and from disadvantaged communities.

PILLAR 3: RESOURCE EFFICIENCY, ENVIRONMENTAL PROTECTION AND CLIMATE CHANGE

One core element of sustainability is a responsible approach to nature, climate and the environment. While unregulated tourism can pose a threat to the environment, well-planned tourism can actually help to protect it – not least when people travel specifically to see rare species or beautiful scenery. Sustainable nature tourism depends upon careful planning and professional assessment of how to protect and preserve habitats. It is also crucial to find ways of ensuring that tourists pay for the resources they use up.

PILLAR 4: CULTURAL VALUES, DIVERSITY AND HERITAGE

Tourists can help to preserve, protect and revitalise traditional cultures, skills and practices. However, it is important to determine what type of tourism and how many tourists are right for the given area. The wishes and culture of the local community must always be taken into account and respected.

PILLAR 5: MUTUAL UNDERSTANDING, PEACE AND SECURITY

Encounters between locals and tourists can contribute to greater understanding and tolerance – which, in turn, can help to make the world a safer and more peaceful place. However, for this to happen, tourism must be structured in a way that facilitates contact with local people and genuine insights into indigenous traditions and culture.

LARGE-SCALE FARMING IN THE CITY

It's a farm. Just not in a form Old MacDonald would recognise. It's in the city, not the countryside, and has no fields, animals, sunlight or rain. It has plants in tightly-packed rows, bathed in bright pink light like a trendy nightclub, and the output of this small space – just 1,000-m² – easily competes with an 80-hectare farm.

The project, by a company called 80 Acres, is an example of how vertical farms – a kind of high-rise urban agriculture – create economic opportunities and drive innovation in cities. They also produce food on a large scale without inflicting damage on nature or depleting resources.

Indoor farming systems like 80 Acres use up to 97% less water than traditional farms. Production in population centres reduces the need for long-distance transport, which saves resources and minimises food waste.

In terms of technology, the main difference between vertical and traditional farms is the use of LED lights. In fields, plants need sunlight to thrive. Vertical farming uses combinations of LED lighting – called light recipes – to grow crops indoors. LED lights are completely different from old-school incandescent lamps, which emitted light as a byproduct of heat when an electrical current ran through a filament. LEDs convert electrical energy directly into photons.

Horticultural and indoor farming systems use the different light frequencies to grow plants with different qualities. For example, a light recipe of 2/3 red and 1/3 blue produces small, dense lettuce heads with reddish, slightly bitter leaves, while 2/3 red and 1/3 green results in a bigger and looser lettuce head, with lighter-coloured, less bitter leaves. The same techniques can also be used on herbs to produce sweeter or spicier notes.

Vertical farming also uses very little energy and no pesticides.

Indoor systems may not replace outdoor farms any time soon, but they do already provide an important supplement to food and the economy in our cities.

MILLIONS IN SLAVERY

Whenever you eat rice or chocolate, buy a mobile phone or new clothes, or grab some fish from the freezer section in your local supermarket, there's a significant risk that slave labour was involved in the production process at some point.

Depriving people of their freedom is one of the most profound violations of human rights, yet the criminal slave trade is lucrative and widespread. It thrives because it preys on the most vulnerable in society, including migrants. The victims usually have very little to lose and no access to legal aid.

According to the Walk Free Foundation's Global Slave Index, 40 million people were living in slavery in 2018 – 71% of them girls and women, often trafficked into prostitution or the victims of forced marriages. Boys and men are often made to work in mines, on fishing boats, or as manual workers on farms and building

sites, sometimes lured by false promises of high wages, only to have their passports taken off them.

The problem may be worst in Africa and Asia but it also plagues the more affluent continents. No country is free from the modern slave trade, for example in the sex industry, and the West imports huge volumes of goods from countries where slave labour is widespread. In 2018, the world's 20 richest countries imported around $354 billion in goods that may well have been tainted by slavery.

According to the Walk Free Foundation, the war on this immoral trade is winnable – but governments, businesses and consumers need to take it seriously. Progress has been made, but the Foundation is encouraging more governments not only to pass anti-slavery legislation but to enforce it and guarantee victims' rights.

Companies and governments also need to demand greater transparency when ordering goods and services. The only way to end slave labour is to draw attention to the millions who have been robbed of their freedom.

08. ACT
COOL IDEAS
OUT OF THE BOX

JOHN MBINDYO INVENTED FRESHBOX
TO HELP HIS LOCAL COMMUNITY, CREATING
NEW OPPORTUNITIES

John Mbindyo was used to the sight – shopkeepers in Nairobi
throwing out all sorts of fruit and vegetables they couldn't
keep fresh in the unrelenting Kenyan heat, either because they
couldn't afford a fridge or didn't have electricity.

"I knew they were losing money, hand over fist, day in, day out.
They didn't know how much – it was just a business cost," he
explains.

The young Kenyan had studied IT but realised he could make
a difference by turning his hand to cooling systems, and the
FreshBox system was born.

FreshBox is a communal cold room, where shopkeepers rent
space by the day, which is far cheaper than buying your own
fridge. Paying by the day also means the system is available
to small businesses that don't have much money. Crucially,
FreshBox is solar-powered, which means it can be used in
areas with no electricity.

"We've democratised the procurement costs so that the
system can also be used in villages or poor neighbourhoods,
and now we're exploring options to bring companies and local
authorities on board as partners," Mbindyo says.

Having grown up in one of the poorest and most violent slums
in Nairobi, Mbindyo has seen the realities of poverty first
hand. By inventing the cooling system, he can create more
opportunities locally as well as help people save money.

"I've always wanted to give something back to the community,
and it makes me really happy to see I'm making a difference."

Mbindyo sees every day as an opportunity. "So many people
have ideas but never get around to putting them into practice.
If we want to make this planet a better place for our children
and grandchildren, we need to dare to take those ideas and
turn them into a reality."

John Mbindyo (left) and co-founders of FreshBox
Daniel Anastos, Forest Redlin and Thomas Schmedding.

GOAL 09

- -

INDUSTRY, INNOVATION AND INFRASTRUCTURE

- -

"LET'S SAVE LIVES – LET'S GO TO WORK.

1,3 million people across the world lose their lives in road accidents every year. It's the leading cause of death among 15 to 29 year olds. Every day 500 children are killed, many on their way to school. This man-made epidemic takes a life every 30 seconds. Road safety is priority target for the UN 2030 Goals. We need safer roads and safer cars, and we have the knowledge. But we need your help and your voice to make the change and save lives. Let's get to work!"

MICHELLE YEOH

Actor, UNDP Goodwill Ambassador and road safety activist

Previous double page: Grande Dixence Dam and Lac des Dix, Val d'Hérémence, Canton of Valais, Switzerland
(46° 05' N – 07° 24' E)

GOAL 09
BUILD RESILIENT INFRASTRUCTURE, PROMOTE SUSTAINABLE INDUSTRIALISATION AND FOSTER INNOVATION

The vision: By 2030, innovation will drive the development of high-quality and reliable infrastructure that supports economic development and human well-being. Small-scale industrial enterprises, in particular in developing countries, will have access to financial services, including affordable credit, and will be integrated into value chains and markets. Scientific research will be enhanced, as will the technological capabilities of industrial sectors in all countries. Innovation will be encouraged. Everyone will be able to access the internet

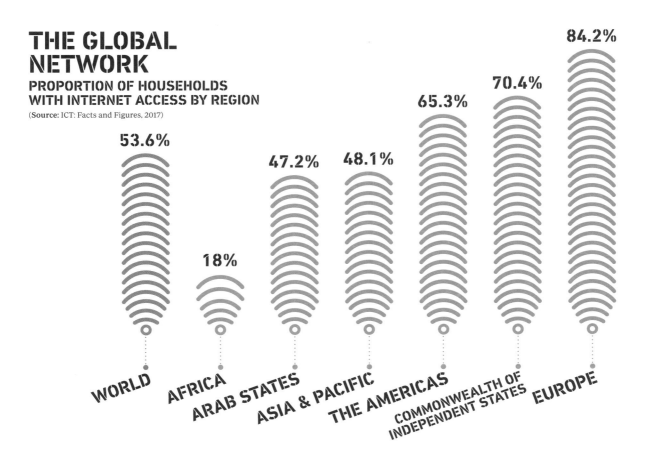

**THE GLOBAL
NETWORK**
PROPORTION OF HOUSEHOLDS
WITH INTERNET ACCESS BY REGION
(**Source:** ICT: Facts and Figures, 2017)

53.6% — WORLD
18% — AFRICA
47.2% — ARAB STATES
48.1% — ASIA & PACIFIC
65.3% — THE AMERICAS
70.4% — COMMONWEALTH OF INDEPENDENT STATES
84.2% — EUROPE

THE ROAD TO PROGRESS

Look around you. How much stuff do you see? Maybe there's a table in front of you, with several objects on it – a coffee cup, a laptop, a notebook, perhaps a vase or pot plant, or a framed photograph of your family? Cast your gaze a little further, and the amount of stuff multiplies exponentially.

Despite living in an age of e-books, music downloads and digital services, manufacturing remains at the heart of international trade and the economy. We produce and consume like never before – and this brings both challenges and opportunities. Globalisation provides developing countries with opportunities for growth, jobs and the prospect of becoming producers in the future. The challenge is how to achieve this while also reducing levels of consumption, reliance on fossil fuels and depletion of natural resources.

Balancing growth and sustainability requires new and more innovative production methods. For the poorest and most isolated parts of the world to benefit from these opportunities will require more than just education and knowledge. First of all, they will need to be connected with the rest of the world.

Without proper roads and reliable means of transport, it is impossible to operate effectively on a large scale. Manufacturing requires a stable energy supply, but vast swathes of sub-Saharan Africa remain off-grid – only one in three households has access to electricity, and many of those choose to go without for reasons of cost. Globally, 1.1 billion people have no electricity, which severely impedes their ability to start or develop their own business.

Manufacturing and trade are also dependent upon the ability to make and receive secure and stable payments – something else that is impossible without electricity. More than half of the people in the world do not have internet access. To compound matters, the gulf continues to widen between the developing world and the technologically advanced nations that manufacture and sell high-tech products at high prices.

In order for everyone to benefit from globalisation and the digital revolution, the most isolated areas must have access to proper roads, electricity, knowledge, investment and the internet. Supply roads are – literally – the road to progress.

09. CREATE
AEROCENE

INITIATED BY TOMÁS SARACENO, THE AEROCENE FOUNDATION IS A NOT-FOR-PROFIT ORGANISATION DEVOTED TO COMMUNITY BUILDING, SCIENTIFIC RESEARCH, ARTISTIC EXPERIENCE, AND EDUCATION

THE TEXT BELOW IS AN ABBREVIATED VERSION OF THE AEROCENE MANIFESTO

AEROCENE MANIFESTO. AERONAUTS UNITE!

While fossil fuel enterprises to colonize other planets are put in place, the air continues to be compromised: how would breathing feel in a post fossil fuel economy, and what is our response-ability? How do we challenge geopolitical borders in an age of climate inequality?

Aerocene imagines space as commons, a physical and imaginative place to be subtracted from corporate control through free access to the atmosphere. The launch pad becomes an aerosolar balloon, a Do It Together (DIT) entrance to the aerial, whose engine is the life-giving star that the extraction of fossil fuels has turned into a threat at a planetary scale. Becoming buoyant and learning how to float compel us to reconsider the ways in which borders are set up by humans, the power of national institutions to decide who can transit, policies that affect vulnerable subjects. *Aerocene* calls for an interspecies right to mobility, a new interplanetary ecology of practice which could reconnect with elemental sources of energy.

A model for a landscape that balances our relationship with, and harnesses the unlimited potential of the Sun. This realisation requires a thermodynamic leap of imagination, just like during an eclipse, when only in the absence of light we become aware of our scale in the shadow of the cosmos.

Researchers in industrial and social ecology refer to "socio-metabolic regimes" to define the epochal

AEROCENE

Aerocene Community, White Sands, New Mexico, 2015, achieving the World Record for the first ever fully-solar manned flight, lifting 7 people for 3h13m. Aerocene is an interdisciplinary artistic endeavor initiated by artist Tomás Saraceno that devises new modes of ecological sensitivity, reactivating a common social imaginary towards an ethical collaboration with the atmosphere and the environment. **Images:** *Aerocene human flight performances*, Ljubljana, on the occasion of the European Days of Mobility, 2018. Next page: *Free Flight Schönefelde*, 2017.

shifts in energetic relationships between humans and their environment, arguing that the first two kinds of metabolic regimes have been solar based, the ones of hunter-gatherer societies and agrarian societies. Today, we are dominated by the fossil fuels regime, mark of the Anthropocene, approaching its end because of the disappearance of the very same energy supplies. What would be the new set of values necessary to overcome the extracting economy of fossil fuel regime? It might it be through a rearticulation of our relationship with the Sun and the cosmos, that we open the boundaries of the Earth to enter an interplanetary-cene.

09. THINK

TECHNOLOGY SHAPES A BRIGHTER FUTURE THAN YOU THINK

RAY KURZWEIL, INVENTOR, AUTHOR, FUTURIST, DESCRIBES IN THIS ESSAY FOR **2030 NOW** HOW TECHNOLOGY IS RAPIDLY CHANGING OUR WORLD FOR THE BETTER

Technologies, he writes, have spawned a virtuous circle advancing every aspect of human well-being, including literacy, education, wealth, health, sanitation, democratisation, and reduction in violence. Due to the exponential growth of technology we will reach a state of prosperity and aboundance within the next three decades that seems almost Utopian today.

I reviewed the extensive positive impact of technological change on social well-being in *The Age of Spiritual Machines* (1999) and *The Singularity is Near* (2005), and in scores of lectures and articles since. In their 2012 book *Abundance*, Peter Diamandis and Steven Kotler fleshed out how we are headed towards an era of abundance in resources that used to be characterised by scarcity. In his 2018 book, *Enlightenment Now*, Steven Pinker describes the continual progress in a variety of areas of social impact.

The exponential growth of technology lies at the core of this progress and will fundamentally improve all aspects of our lives in the very near future. The exponential curve is about to become steep and will transform areas we do not normally consider to be information technologies, such as food, clothing and

housing, even land use. Life is getting exponentially better and the future is brighter than you think.

So why is there popular misconception that things are getting worse? Readers of news stories are attracted to, well, stories.

A story starts with a challenge that generally represents bad news. The problem typically grows more acute and is resolved at the end in a "resurrection". This is the paradigm that the news tries to emulate, although these stories rarely get to the resolution part, as the news is continually launching into new stories with more bad news.

Our attraction to bad news is also an evolutionary adaptation. It was more important for survival to pay attention to potential challenges – to note the rustling in the leaves that might be a predator, than the fact that your crops may be 0.1% better than last year.

Vertical farming, like here in the projected ReGen Village outside Amsterdam by Danish architects EFFEKT, can help ensure a sustainable future food production.

"THE REALITY IS THAT EVERY ASPECT OF LIFE IS GETTING PROGRESSIVELY BETTER AS A RESULT OF EXPONENTIALLY IMPROVING TECHNOLOGY"

RAY KURZWEIL, INVENTOR, FUTURIST

Another well-documented evolutionary adaptation is our psychological bias towards remembering the past as better than it was. Memories of pain and distress fade more quickly than positive memories. When we look back on our past experiences, the pain, stresses and challenges have faded, and we tend to remember the more positive aspects of life.

Conversely, when we think of the present, we are highly cognisant of our current worries and difficulties. This leads to the often-false impression that the past was better than the present, despite overwhelming objective evidence to the contrary.

As one of many examples of this phenomenon, a 2016 survey asked 26,000 people in 24 countries, speaking 15 languages and accounting for 62% of the world's population, whether or not worldwide poverty had increased or decreased, and by how much. 87% thought poverty had increased, and only 13% responded correctly that poverty had decreased in the past 20 years. Only 1% correctly answered that it had decreased by more than 50%.

The reality is that every aspect of life is getting progressively better as a result of exponentially improving technology. Technology, both

communication and production technologies, have spawned a virtuous circle that advances every aspect of human well-being, including literacy, education, wealth, health, sanitation, democratisation and reduction in violence.

In 1800, scarcely 1 in 10 people worldwide could read. Today, the worldwide literacy rate exceeds 86%, and developed countries often boast figures above 99%. In 1870, the population of the United States had an average of just over four years of education, and by 2010 this had increased to over 13 years.

Since 2000, the percentage of the world's children estimated to be in hazardous work has fallen from 11.1% to 4.6%. A thousand years ago, life expectancy at birth was in the 20s, and in 1800 it was only 37. Today, we have doubled that number.

As all industries – energy, manufacturing, farming, health and medicine, etc. – become information technologies, they are subject to the Law of Accelerating Returns, i.e. the doubling of capability (for the same cost) each year.

For example, the genome project was a perfect exponential doubling in price-performance and capacity each year, and this progression has continued since the completion of the project in 2003. The method of developing new health treatments has changed from a linear hit-or-miss process to an exponential information technology, in which we are systematically reprogramming the suboptimal software of life. The trickle of clinical applications today will become a flood during the 2020s.

We are beginning now to use AI, Artificial Intelligence, for both drug and intervention discovery and design, and by the end of the 2020s biological simulators will enable us to do clinical trials in hours rather than years. As a result, the linear models of progress in medicine and longevity will no longer be appropriate. Awareness that radical life extension is close at hand is spreading, but most people, both doctors and patients, are still unaware of this grand transformation in our ability to reprogram our outdated biology.

Another powerful example is the impact of exponentially advancing communication technologies on the spread of modern democracy from its roots in medieval England. In 1900, fewer than 12% of the world's population lived in democracies, but that climbed to just under 20% by 1922. With the breakup of the Soviet Union, democracy again expanded rapidly, reaching 57% of the world's population by 2002.

In 1999, 30% of the world's population lived in autocracies – the most repressive class of regime. By 2015, this figure was down to 23%. The challenge over the coming decades will be to help countries in the grey area between autocracy and democracy make the transition to fully democratic governance.

With multiple transformations, first in mass communication and recently in personalised media, the ideas of democracy and individual rights have become accepted worldwide as desirable goals. This was not the case two centuries ago, and was barely acknowledged one century ago.

In an onstage dialogue with Christine LaGarde, Managing Director of the International Monetary Fund, and other economic leaders at the IMF's Annual Meeting on 5 October 2016, LaGarde asked me why we don't see more evidence of economic growth from all of the remarkable digital technology. My answer was (and is) that we factor it out by putting it in both the numerator and denominator. When a teenager in Africa spends $50 on a smartphone, it counts for $50 of economic activity, despite the fact that it is equivalent to a billion dollars of computation and communication technology circa 1965, millions of dollars circa 1985.

We completely ignore the steep deflation rate for information technology – which in the case of computation, communication, genetic sequencing, etc., is in the order of 50% per year. We assign part of this constant improvement to price, the other part to performance, so we get ever better products for lower prices. For example, today, your cell phone is hundreds of thousands of times more powerful and almost a million times less expensive than the computer that I used as a student at MIT in 1965.

One common criticism is that while digital technology has many remarkable qualities and implications, you can't eat it, you can't wear it and you can't live in it. My response is that this is all going to change over the next decade.

We are now entering an era in which food, clothing and shelter are not simply being made more economical due to information technology but are literally *becoming* information technologies. They

will, therefore, be subject to the same high deflation rates that we see for other information technologies. We will print out clothing with 3D printers, ultimately for pennies. We will produce food using vertical agriculture, with AI-controlled food production and harvesting of high-quality, affordable food, free from chemicals.

We will produce the physical things we need, including modules to snap together houses and buildings – also at low cost. These are all capabilities that have been demonstrated and will be mainstream in the 2020s.

Many products won't even need a physical form at all, as simulated versions will perform perfectly well in highly realistic virtual and augmented reality – for example, a full virtual environment, complete with seemingly physical objects with which we can have visual, auditory, and tactile interactions. We will increasingly utilise unused land by living where we want while continuing to be able to work and play together via highly convincing virtual and augmented reality technologies.

Throughout history, the physical essentials of life have formed the basis of competition. As we enter an era of abundance and the availability of material needs becomes universal, the struggle will be for purpose and meaning. The transcendent things that we can do with life – creating and appreciating artistic works, expressing a loving sentiment, sharing humour – are what gives life meaning.

These abilities will be greatly enhanced as we extend our neocortex in the cloud, using medical nanorobots that will enter the brain through the capillaries and provide wireless communication between our neocortical modules and the cloud.

Just as your smartphone today amplifies its capabilities by connecting to many computers in the cloud, we will do the same thing with our neocortex. This is a 2030s and 2040s scenario. Our thinking then will become a hybrid of the biological and the nonbiological in the cloud. As a result, we will become smarter, more musical, funnier, etc.

While the social and philosophical ramifications of these changes will be profound, and the threats they pose considerable, we will ultimately merge with our machines, live indefinitely, and be a billion times more intelligent – all within the next three decades.

09. ACT
WE ARE ALL DESIGNING OUR FUTURE

"MOST OF THE WORLD'S PROBLEMS ARE DOWN TO DESIGN," SAYS **LEYLA ACAROGLU**, DESIGNER, SOCIOLOGIST AND SUSTAINABILITY PROVOCATEUR, "AND DESIGN WILL SOLVE THEM TOO"

It all began when Leyla, a 20 year-old design student at the time, first encountered the Gaia theory. Already passionate about human rights and inequality, and a self-confessed "bit of a rebel", her worldview shifted dramatically as the teacher explained how everything is interconnected. It marked the beginning of her understanding that design needs to be based on a holistic, interconnected approach.

"Looking at problems in isolation often leads to solutions that just lead to trouble further down the line," she explains.

According to Dr Acaroglu, design will be crucial to achieving the UN 2030 Goals. Design is, in the broadest sense, the script for our life on Earth. We shape it through our design, but that design shapes us in turn.

"We need solutions that make it easy to make sustainable choices. We need to understand complex interconnections and incorporate them into our solutions," she says.

"Our current 'take-make-waste' approach to design is at the heart of the problems that we face. The upside is that we have the capacity to design ourselves out of these problems, if we change the way we think. Through our actions, each and every one of us is a designer of the future. Our choices determine how the future will look."

When not travelling the world teaching new ways of thinking about design, she often spends time in Portugal, where she is helping to restore an old olive and citrus farm on a sustainable basis.

"Through this project, I am learning more about the natural systems that we, as designers, need to work with. We live on an isolated planet with limited resources. If we design according to the same principles as nature, nothing will go to waste."

Leyla Acaroglu, one of the world's most innovative environmentalists, at her farm in Portugal which serves as a creative workshop for sustainable solutions and practices.

10 REDUCED
INEQUALITIES

GOAL 10

REDUCED INEQUALITIES

"I'M A DAD. LIKE ALL PARENTS, I WANT MY CHILDREN AND GRANDCHILDREN TO GROW UP IN A BETTER, FAIRER, SAFER AND CLEANER WORLD.

But I fear that may not be possible, that we have been too greedy in our exploitation of the world's resources. But it's not too late. We can turn things around, we can create a better world – together. The 17 global goals are extremely ambitious. And they need to be. For as long as children are dying of hunger; as long as people are discriminated against because of race, religion or sexuality; as long as millions of people are fleeing the horrors of war; as long as animal and plant species are being wiped out; as long as the climate continues to change beyond recognition, then we have not done enough. There is no alternative"

NIKOLAJ COSTER-WALDAU

Actor and UNDP Goodwill Ambassador

GOAL 10
REDUCE INEQUALITY WITHIN AND AMONG COUNTRIES

The vision: By 2030 the income gap between the poorest 40% and the rest of the population will have narrowed. All people will have equal opportunities. Inequalities will be reduced and discriminatory laws, policies and practices will be eliminated. Instead, policies that promote equality will be in place. Developing countries will have stronger voices in global institutions, in order to deliver more effective, credible and legitimate institutions. Migration policies will facilitate orderly, safe, regular and responsible migration and mobility of people

A GLOBAL MOVEMENT

MORE PEOPLE MIGRATE, BUT THE MIGRANTS' SHARE OF THE TOTAL POPULATION IS RELATIVELY STABLE

(**Source:** International Organization for Migration (IOM): World Migration Report 2018)

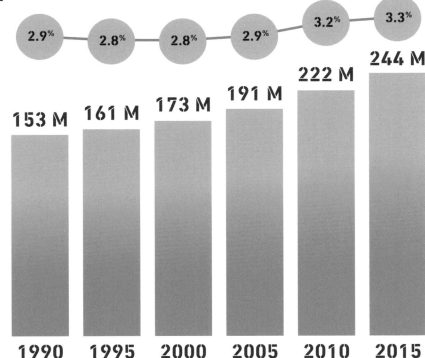

2.9% 2.8% 2.8% 2.9% 3.2% 3.3%

153 M 161 M 173 M 191 M 222 M 244 M

1990 1995 2000 2005 2010 2015

MIGRANTS – INDISPENSABLE AND UNWELCOME

Migrants have some of the best jobs – and the worst. Some enjoy privileges in their host countries – others suffer abuse, discrimination and harassment. Some earn sky-high salaries – others scrape by in precarious jobs outside the system.

What migrants have in common is that they move to other countries in search of a better life and to improve their prospects.

The best-educated people in the world are in huge demand in many sectors and nations. Competition for their services is so fierce that countries often offer them tax breaks and other incentives. The reality is, however, that the majority of migrants are among the most vulnerable groups in society. While some are refugees and asylum seekers fleeing war or persecution, many more, numbering in the millions, are simply seeking a better life for themselves and their families.

The number of migrants continues to rise. Migration in search of a better life is often seen as a problem, but the reality is far more complex. In countries and regions with labour shortages, migrants are indispensable. The money they send home is also often substantially more than their native countries receive in various forms of international development aid.

Migrants contribute to the prosperity of both host and home country, but often encounter hostility from people who view them as a threat to their own job security and social safety net, or view migrant culture with suspicion. Many developed countries apply strict rules on migrant labour that discriminate against certain groups.

Improved and better-regulated conditions and guaranteed rights for migrants are crucial prerequisites for reducing global inequality. In turn, less global inequality will enable many more people to achieve a high quality of life in their home country, hopefully turning migration into a choice rather than a necessity in the future.

10. CREATE
AI WEIWEI

"THE REFUGEE CRISIS IS NOT ABOUT REFUGEES, RATHER, IT IS ABOUT US. OUR PRIORITISATION OF FINANCIAL GAIN OVER PEOPLE'S STRUGGLE FOR THE NECESSITIES OF LIFE IS THE PRIMARY CAUSE OF MUCH OF THIS CRISIS"

They sit crammed together on a giant life raft. Hundreds of anonymous figures. Men, women, children.

We are familiar with the scene from the news. People crossing borders and braving dangerous waters in the hope of finding safety and a better future on the other side. But in Ai Weiwei's art installation *Law of the Journey*, everything has been magnified. Simply turning it off or looking the other way is not an option. There are hundreds of them – some of them dead or dying.

We call them migrants. But we should call them displaced, says Chinese artist and activist Ai Weiwei, whose work in recent years has explored what it means to be a refugee. This has included art installations in which prominent buildings were covered with thousands of lifejackets used by those fleeing across the Mediterranean, as well as the documentary *Human Flow*. For the film, Weiwei visited 23 countries and more than 40 refugee camps. It was shortlisted for Best Documentary at the 2018 Oscars.

"Instead of building walls, we should look at what is causing people to become refugees and work to solve those conditions to stem the flow at its source," says Ai Weiwei. He is critical of the West for abandoning the ideals set out in declarations on universal human rights, in favour of short-sighted greed and cowardice.

The UN Sustainable Development Goal for reduced inequality can only be reached if the richest countries and the richest people acknowledge their responsibility for including all, the most vulnerable not least, in a fairer distribution of wealth and resources.

Ai Weiwei is himself a refugee. When he was a child, his family was expelled from China's capital, Beijing. He knows first-hand what it is to grow up in a camp, robbed of dignity and humanity, constantly exposed to hatred and discrimination. Weiwei has devoted much of his adult life to campaigning for human rights.

"There have always been people who are unfortunate or victimised by those who profit from the established system. Only by creating an understanding that humanity is one – that it needs to be shared and protected by everyone – can we begin to improve this situation," explains Ai Weiwei. He asks for more compassion when it comes to the plight of refugees. The number of displaced people globally is at a record high and has been labelled a refugee crisis. It is not, says Ai Weiwei. It is a crisis of humanity.

AI WEIWEI

Chinese contemporary artist, active in sculpture, installation, architecture, curating, photography, social media and film, as well as a political activist. **Artwork:** *Law of the Journey*, 2017. Installation view at the National Gallery in Prague, 2017.

10. THINK INEQUALITY IS A GLOBAL PROBLEM

THE NUMBER OF PEOPLE LIVING IN POVERTY MAY BE FALLING, BUT THE GAP BETWEEN THE WEALTHIEST 10% AND THE POOREST 40% IS WIDENING

The annual Credit Suisse Global Wealth Report provides statistics on income, purchasing power, savings, shares, land ownership, property and other assets. According to the latest report, the richest 1% own 47% of total global wealth. The rest is shared among the remaining 99% of us. The top 10% own 85% of the world's riches.

What does it take to get into the top 1%? According to Credit Suisse, an annual income of approximately $900,000. About $93,000 will put you in the top 10%, and anything over $4,200 p.a. makes you wealthier than half of your fellow human beings.

Broadly speaking, economic growth is a success story – every day, more than 130,000 people are lifted out of extreme poverty. While everybody benefited from this growth prior to 2008/2009, inequality has increased substantially since the crash. The wealthiest have been the main beneficiaries of subsequent recoveries on the financial markets. Others have seen their finances stagnate or even deteriorate.

The latest Credit Suisse report suggests that this trend may be slowing, but economic inequality – both within and between countries – remains strong, and creates unrest and inequality in other spheres. The British health researcher and author Kate Pickett has written a number of books on inequality and how it affects standards of living in various ways.

HEALTH: Financially unequal countries have a lower life expectancy and a higher incidence of certain diseases and conditions, including obesity, infant mortality and mental disorders – and it's not just the poor who suffer. In unequal societies, the richest people have poorer health than the affluent in more equal societies. Studies have shown that inequality leads to higher levels of stress, greater insecurity and less social cohesion – factors that affect rich and poor alike.

SOCIAL COHESION: In severely unequal countries, social mobility is far more restricted than in countries with greater equality. According to the Organisation for Economic Cooperation and Development (OECD), it takes on average five generations for a poor British family to climb the social ladder and earn an average income. In more equal countries, like Denmark, it takes two generations. According to the OECD, Colombia has the worst social mobility – it takes 11 generations. In unequal societies, crime is more rife, women have lower social and economic status, and discrimination against minorities is more widespread.

CHILD DEVELOPMENT: In unequal societies, more children fail to develop properly – socially, mentally and physically – and perform poorly at school. Teenage pregnancy is much more prevalent, more children drop out of school, and more young people become involved in crime.

SUSTAINABLE GROWTH: According to the American inequality researcher Professor Robert H. Frank, status symbols are in greater demand in unequal societies, and many more people accumulate debt, which makes it difficult to redistribute wealth for the common good and restrict consumption. Political and business leaders in these countries also tend to be less interested in the climate, environment and nature.

In other words, there are plenty of reasons to be concerned about inequality, above and beyond whether you think it's unfair or not. It makes societies unstable, ratchets up discrimination, impacts on everybody's health, and makes it difficult to plan and invest in collective and sustainable solutions.

BASIC INCOME — A WAY FORWARD?

Imagine being given a basic amount to live on, no matter whether you're unemployed, a student or outside the labour market for some other reason. The concept of universal basic income (UBI) is brought up more and more often as a potential solution to inequality and to the large number of jobs sacrificed on the altar of digitalisation.

Strong welfare states like the Nordic countries spend large sums on various forms of unemployment benefit, much of it on control measures to check that the recipients meet strict eligibility rules. In theory, UBI would slash admin costs and empower people to unleash their creativity and altruism – as artists, entrepreneurs, volunteers and so on.

Just as importantly, it would significantly reduce inequality by ensuring that every single one of us, regardless of background or circumstances, would have enough money to live on. This would especially benefit women, who tend to be among the world's poorest and carry out large amounts of unpaid labour.

The problem is that provisional evaluations of the system have proved inconclusive. For example,

Luke Martinelli, a researcher at the University of Bath in the UK, concluded that "affordable UBI would be inadequate, and an adequate UBI would be unaffordable".

Others disagree. They see it as an obvious way of making society more dynamic and fair. Advocates claim it would eliminate the stigma sometimes associated with benefits, because it would be a universal right and not means-tested.

Another advantage is that it would allow people in low-paid jobs or with little to no education to retrain or upskill. It would also make it easier to relocate to find work – people wouldn't be as geographically restricted as they currently are in most parts of the world. Business would also benefit from a higher-quality and more highly motivated workforce.

One of the most common counterarguments is that basic income would discourage large numbers of people from working. Pilot schemes suggest otherwise. The fall in numbers in work is negligible and the numbers in education and training, including teenagers, tends to increase.

Basic income is still controversial, and researchers are keen to stress that it isn't a panacea. Nonetheless, it is rapidly making its way up the political agenda.

10 ACT
KOKETSO MOETI: SUDDENLY WE HAD POWER

Koketso Moeti, stresses that activism is not just about victories. It's about the long haul and changing attitudes, and anybody can contribute.

"NEW TECHNOLOGY IS TOO IMPORTANT TO LEAVE TO MARKET FORCES ALONE"

KOKETSO MOETI, FOUNDER, AMANDLA.MOBI

Rooigrond is the sort of small town that most people just drive through. It has few attractions – in fact, its most prominent landmark is a prison. Isolated in the north-west of the country, it usually takes an escape for the village to hit the headlines. But not in 2012.

The villagers had spent six years fighting to stay on land most of them were settled on by the government, after the 1994 elections when South Africa became a democracy. On the day that the new constitution was signed, white farmers fired large numbers of black labourers, but the government gave them permission to stay and work the red soil from which Rooigrond takes its name.

In 2006, the local council changed all that. It drew up plans to redevelop Rooigrond – but the settlers were in the way. The intention was to resettle them elsewhere, but they refused, heralding the start of a long, drawn-out dispute, during which the villagers had their supplies of water, fuel and other necessities cut off.

One of the villagers was a young woman, Koketso Moeti, the daughter of an anti-apartheid activist. Unlike most other local women, she was English literate. Moeti had seen how the new social media platforms could be used to spread messages, and how protesters could use mobile phones to co-ordinate events, share information and make their voices heard.

"Suddenly we had power. We were listened to. We were no longer just 1,500 people, cut off from the world, fighting on our own," says Moeti, who became the driving force behind "Operation Rooigrond". More than just a protest, it was a struggle that bound the community together and led to the setting up of things like a meeting house, a library and a communal kitchen. By sharing their story on social media, the locals raised awareness of their plight far beyond South Africa's borders, and support flooded in.

By 2012, the pressure on the local government had become so great that the people of Rooigrond were granted the right to stay, but for Moeti it wasn't the end of the line. She developed the Amandla.mobi platform, which now boasts over 200,000 active users and serves as an effective tool in the struggle for justice and against inequality in South Africa – or Mzansi, a colloquial name for the country.

Users of the platform run campaigns, spread information, mobilise and generate support. All they need is a mobile phone – which the vast majority of people in South Africa have.

"Our fight against forced resettlement made me reflect on how technology had amplified our voices. People who were used to being ignored could now tell their stories. Together, we were strong. It became clear to me that we had to apply our experience to other issues and allow others to be heard as well. It was too important – we couldn't just rest on our laurels," she says.

Moeti was recently chosen as one of 20 participants in former US President Barack Obama's Fellowship programme. She is often described as an entrepreneur and app developer, but her focus is not on the technology in itself, but on what it does for people.

"We sometimes speak in awestruck terms about new technology and flashy things like AI, but using technology to boost activism is nothing new," she says.

"The arrival of the printing press enabled people to produce banners and posters to spread their messages more rapidly. The internet made it possible to share news even faster and more widely. Turning the mobile phone into a campaigning tool was a natural next step," she explains.

For Moeti, it is crucial that the new technologies are used to build and empower communities, to give a voice to those who have traditionally been ignored – and that requires an active effort.

"Otherwise, we leave technology in the hands of people who want to exploit it commercially. It is far too important for us to let that happen."

As well as its near-universalism, another major advantage of the mobile phone is that everybody can use it, no matter how good their English. South Africa has 11 official languages. For many of its people, English is only their second or third language.

"It can be difficult to make yourself heard if you don't have good English. But with a mobile phone, this isn't an issue. Anyone can send a message, and Amandla. mobi helps to set up campaigns," Moeti explains. Not all campaigns succeed. For example, Amandla. mobi was used to fight against the forced relocation of a group of mentally ill patients from a specialist hospital to private charitable institutions. However,

the relocation went ahead, and at least 144 patients – more than one in ten – died of thirst, hunger, lack of medicine or other forms of neglect when the private institutions proved incapable of providing them with the requisite care.

"We failed to prevent the forced relocation. It's difficult to generate sympathy for psychiatric patients, as a lot of people say that they don't contribute anything to society. But we witnessed their suffering. We were there to support their families. We made sure that the victims weren't invisible – and in doing so, we raised awareness about people suffering from mental illness."

Moeti believes that activism all too often focuses on visible victories and elevating visible individuals as if they are the only ones on the frontline.

"But when we strengthen local society and our communities, it is about much more than that. It's about the unseen people who enable what those who are visible do. Like in my case, the people who look after my kids while I attend events. Activism that builds people up and changes attitudes is crucial, even if some types are less visible than others. When people act together, in co-operation, bringing whatever they have to offer, things happen, and I find hope again, even though I have my moments of pessimism," she adds.

"Activism isn't something you just take or leave, like a job. It's the way that you live. You have to try and live your life according to your ideals. Nothing comes from nothing, and that includes Amandla.mobi. We stand on the shoulders of those who fought before us. It is now our duty to think about how we can be the shoulders on which future generations stand."

SUSTAINABLE CITIES AND COMMUNITIES

"I BELIEVE THE CITY IS CIVILISATION'S GREATEST CREATION AND ITS MOST INTRIGUING ONGOING DILEMMA.

My approach to architecture has always been rooted in an empathic relationship to local context. Sustainability is not a clip-on badge, but is an understanding of the specificities of geography, climate and culture. I've also come to realise that to keep pace with the runaway growth of cities, we need to think beyond a global perception to a truly planetary conceptualisation of our world. Therefore, for us to really grasp sustainability in the 21st century, we need to harness, mobilise and align ourselves from the local to the planetary"

SIR DAVID ADJAYE OBE

Architect, Principal of Adjaye Associates
and the lead designer of the National Museum of African American History and Culture

Previous double page: Cyclists at a 2030 NOW event in Copenhagen, one of the most bicycle-friendly capital cities in the world. Israels Plads, Copenhagen, Denmark (55° 40' 58" N – 12° 34' 06" E)

GOAL 11
MAKE CITIES AND HUMAN SETTLEMENTS INCLUSIVE, SAFE, RESILIENT AND SUSTAINABLE

The vision: By 2030 all countries will have adequate, safe and affordable housing, basic services and sustainable transport systems. Public transport will be expanded, with an emphasis on the needs of the vulnerable, women, children, people with disabilities and older people. Urbanisation will be inclusive and sustainable, with clean air and responsible waste management, resilient to climate change and natural catastrophes, and everyone will have access to safe green and public spaces. Greater efforts will be made to protect and preserve the world's cultural and natural heritage

THE BRIGHT CITY LIGHTS

THE URBAN POPULATION IS GROWING MAINLY DUE TO NATURAL POPULATION GROWTH AND MIGRATION FROM RURAL AREAS.

(**Source:** UN: World Urbanization Prospects, 2014)

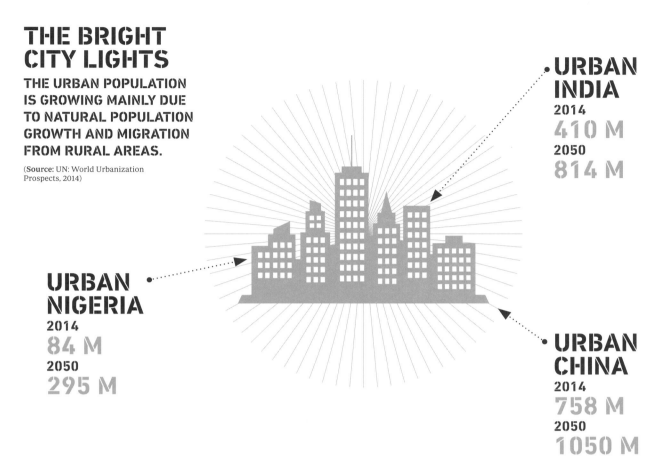

URBAN INDIA
2014
410 M
2050
814 M

URBAN NIGERIA
2014
84 M
2050
295 M

URBAN CHINA
2014
758 M
2050
1050 M

CITIES – KEY TO SUSTAINABILITY

The rate of inward migration from rural to urban areas has never been so rapid. The shift, which began in earnest during the Industrial Revolution, has gained new momentum. The world's cities are growing at a rate of one million new inhabitants every five days. According to projections, 60% of the global population is expected to live in urban areas by 2030 – and all the indications are that this trend will only accelerate.

Urban population growth makes cities the key to sustainable development. It is crucial that they grow in ways that make them safe and healthy places to live. As things stand, many urban areas are bursting. They occupy just 3% of the land but are already home to half of the world's population and account for up to 80% of energy use. This massive concentration of people and resources places huge demands on planning.

According to the UN, 95% of urban growth is concentrated in developing countries, which have found it difficult to rise to the planning challenge.

A lack of sewage systems, housing and public transport, combined with poor or inadequate supplies of water and energy, and an absence of traffic planning, are leading to huge cities in which disease, pollution and accidents kill people and exacerbate health problems and poverty. More than 800 million people live in slums without even the most basic facilities. To stop this figure rising, we must bring the urbanisation process under control and plan safe and healthy cities.

On the other hand, intense concentrations of people also afford opportunities for greater efficiency and innovation in our use of resources. With so many different skills and functions in one place, cities serve as hubs for new and better solutions.

Urban economic growth is important, but if cities are to fulfil their potential to help make the future more sustainable, they must focus on the quality of life, the environment and how they use resources.

11. CREATE
AGNES DENES

"LOOKING BACK ON MY WORK, I NOW SEE THAT EACH ONE OF THEM IS TRYING TO HELP HUMANITY WITH A MAJOR PROBLEM, OFFERING BENIGN SOLUTIONS"

Agnes Denes began working with landscapes in the 1960s, at a time when scant attention was being paid to nature and the environment, and the rampant rise of prosperity, especially in the West, was encroaching on and inflicting damage on both.

Her first artistic endeavours were in painting, trying out at least six or seven different techniques before breaking through the canvas and out into the environment. Since then, she has worked in a range of different media – from huge landscape projects to poetry and drawings of scientific and philosophical principles – but the encounter between the artificial and the natural is a constant leitmotif.

Nature has a life of its own, of course, but we shape it and bring our ability to think in intellectual, abstract and mathematical terms to bear on it. According to Denes, we should use that ability to promote sustainability. Her "Future Cities" series, now more than 40 years old, presents an imaginary world in which cities are self-sufficient and able to withstand climate change. They are also witty and magnificent.

Her 1982 work, *Wheatfield – A Confrontation*, is a ground-breaking example of landscape art. For one summer, it was the wheat field with the most expensive address in the world, close to Wall Street on Manhattan, with the iconic twin towers of the World Trade Centre and the Statue of Liberty as its backdrop. "*Wheatfield* was a symbol, a universal concept; it represented food, energy, commerce, world trade and economics.

AGNES DENES

A pioneer of ecological art and a primary figure among the concept-based artists who emerged in the 1960s and 1970s, New York-based Agnes Denes is internationally known for works created in a wide range of media. **Artworks:** *Wheatfield – A Confrontation*, 1982. Next page: *The Living Pyramid*, 2015.

It referred to mismanagement, waste, greed, world hunger and ecological concerns," she writes.

Denes and a small group of volunteers sowed the seeds of the golden grain in a former landfill site. Originally commissioned to produce a sculpture, she decided that the world already had more than enough public sculptures, especially "public sculptures with men sitting on horses".

The wheat field has since been replaced by a whole new district: the steel, glass and concrete of Battery Park City. Before that, it was harvested, yielding half a ton of grain – a precursor to the key role of "urban farming" in modern, sustainable cities. The grain then travelled to 28 cities around the globe where people took away small packets to plant in solidarity with her concepts.

11. THINK
TWO WHEELS,
NINE GOALS

FAST, EFFICIENT, HEALTHY AND INEXPENSIVE – CYCLING HAS
SO MANY POSITIVE ASPECTS THAT HELP US PURSUE MORE
THAN HALF OF THE UN 2030 GOALS

At the peak of the rush hour, traffic pours out onto the roads of Denmark's capital, Copenhagen. But it's not the car that dominates. No matter the purpose of the trip or the destination, the bike is the preferred mode of transport for the locals, who collectively cover 1.36 million km per day – the equivalent of circumnavigating the globe 34 times.

Civil servants and businesspeople in pinstriped suits ride bikes with boxes for their kids, dropping them off at nursery on the way to work. School pupils, students, shop assistants... during the morning rush hour, the whole of Copenhagen seems to pass you by on two wheels. It doesn't really matter what time of year it is – in winter the most important cycle paths are cleared of snow and ice before the roads. Without bikes, the transport system would grind to a halt. Copenhagen's cycling culture is one of the main reasons that the city consistently ranks as one of the best places in the world to live.

Bikes change the nature of urban life. In heavy city traffic, they are often the quickest way to get around. The regional authority operates on the basis that the use of bikes keeps thousands of cars off the roads. A cycling culture is also good for the economy. Traffic congestion wastes time, lowers productivity and

deters people from looking for work any further away than necessary from where they live.

Cycling also has other benefits for the local and national bottom line. Cyclists are healthier than drivers, which means 1.1 million fewer sick days p.a. across the region. Exercise enhances the ability to concentrate. Studies show that children learn better when they walk or cycle to school. Cycling has environmental benefits – it is carbon-neutral and generates no noise or air pollution. It's also inexpensive. Not everybody can afford a car and all of the accompanying costs (petrol, maintenance, insurance, parking, etc.), but most people can afford a bike.

Urban planners across the world are also realising that the bike solves multiple problems at once. Many cities were once filled with bikes, but cars or scooters replaced them as people became more affluent. Indeed, the bike was often seen as a symbol of poverty.

But studies have shown that cycling helps generate revenue in poorer countries and regions. In fact, as a mode of transport, the bike is part of the solution to a number of the UN 2030 Goals – not just no. 11 on sustainable cities. Here is how the bicycle contributes toward some of the other goals:

GOAL 01
NO POVERTY

Many developing countries just do not have public transport in rural areas, and people simply cannot afford cars. They have to get around on foot instead. A lot of time is spent walking to and from work and school, going shopping, collecting water, etc. Not only do bikes cover more ground faster, but they let people carry far more than they can on foot – leaving more time to spend on school, on studies or on looking for work farther afield. A bike makes it easier to run a business and to collect and deliver goods more quickly.

An experiment involving small dairy farms in Zambia showed an average increase in income of 23% when the farmers were given access to bikes. The milk made it to the dairy more quickly, more could be transported at once, and the milk was fresher, meaning that less of it was discarded.

GOAL 02
ZERO HUNGER

Bikes make it possible to collect and deliver food more quickly, cutting the level of waste. Food security improves when you deliver and collect more food at once, and when you can travel farther to buy and sell it.

GOAL 03
GOOD HEALTH AND WELL-BEING

Cycling is both a form of exercise and saves the environment from air and noise pollution. In rural areas, the poorest are able to visit a doctor or health centre by bike. This saves time compared with walking, leaving more time for leisure with friends and family.

GOAL 04
QUALITY EDUCATION

Danish studies have shown that children who walk or cycle to school are better able to concentrate. In areas where walking is the only way for poor people to get around, a bike makes it possible to travel farther and allows more time for collecting food and water, studying and doing homework.

Studies from rural areas in Zimbabwe show that absenteeism from school falls sharply when the students cycle and that almost twice as many students with bikes pass their exams than those without.

GOAL 05
GENDER EQUALITY

In many of the rural areas in developing nations, women do the cleaning and shopping and collect the firewood and water. On foot, this takes up much of the day, leaving precious little time for study or work. Girls and women are effectively chained to the home. Bikes free up time for school and studying, and girls with an education go on to earn more money and have fewer children. Often, cycling is also a safer way for women and girls to get around than on foot.

GOAL 06
CLEAN WATER AND SANITATION

One in nine people in the world do not live near a supply of clean drinking water. Fetching drinking water by foot is time-consuming, and you can't carry as much as you need. Bikes solve both of these problems, allowing people to carry more water over greater distances.

GOAL 10
REDUCED INEQUALITIES

Cycling lets the poorest people travel greater distances for education and work, and to reach bigger markets for buying and selling goods.

GOAL 12
RESPONSIBLE CONSUMPTION AND PRODUCTION

Cycling is an environmentally and climate-friendly form of transport that doesn't rely on fossil fuels and doesn't emit CO_2 or other pollutants.

HIGH-RISE URBAN GARDEN

The Chippendale district in Sydney was once known for its industry, its brewery and "Pig Mary" – a woman who, like so many others afflicted by poverty in the 19th century, did whatever it took to get by. Pig Mary, whose real name was Mary O'Shea, survived by collecting offal from abattoirs.

Contemporary Chippendale is a far cry from that darker past and is rapidly earning a name for its spectacular, sustainable high-rise buildings – most notably One Central Park, which has won awards for innovation. All of the water here – from rainwater to wastewater – is recirculated, and the district is on course to be Australia's most sustainable, as new buildings using the latest solutions spring up all of the time.

It isn't the technology that is the most striking feature though. Entirely covered in greenery, One Central Park looks like a vertical garden. It is home to almost 40,000 plants – indigenous Australian species and more exotic varieties. The plants cool the building, absorb air pollution and keep the noise down. Studies have also shown that green surroundings enhance our overall well-being. A huge platform juts out near the top of one of the two blocks. On top is a park, while the mirrored underside reflects light on to the plants and flats below. After dark, an array of LEDs turns the platform into a work of art.

One Central Park is just one of many new buildings designed to combine sustainability, technology and simple, low-tech solutions like planting more trees and plants. Not only does the greenery provide shade, cooling and protection from pollution, it also provides a defence against flooding during heavy downpours.

Several other cities are also working on large rooftop parks, e.g. the high-rise "urban farms" growing cabbage and lettuce springing up in Shanghai. Building vertically instead of horizontally makes efficient use of valuable space – an absolute necessity in our ever-growing cities.

Opposite page: *One Central Park*, Sydney.

THOSE LEFT BEHIND

No one knows the exact figure, but the Chinese authorities estimate that around nine million children in the Chinese countryside have grown up without their parents.

They're not orphans, although in some ways they might as well be, because their parents aren't there. They left for the cities to work and earn money, but couldn't take their children with them, partly because of legislation that only guaranteed schooling and medical care in the area where they were born. The children have been left with other relatives, usually grandparents, but in practice many are left to fend for themselves. Often, the oldest sibling takes on the role as head of the family.

Their parents may have left to build a better future for their children, but studies have shown that children separated from their parents often face greater problems in school and life in general.

It is not only in China that children are left behind like this, although that is where the phenomenon has received the most attention. In other countries, too, parents have little choice but to head to the cities to earn a living, either in their home country or abroad.

Often, this exodus also leaves a lot of older people isolated. In many countries, multi-generational living used to be commonplace, or at least families lived close to each other in rural communities. The younger generation would typically take over the farm or other family business once their parents were too old to work. In return, the older generation looked after the grandkids.

That way of life is disappearing. Younger people are flocking to the cities in larger numbers, in search of an education and better jobs, leaving many older people cut off from their families. Rural depopulation also leads to shops closing and cuts to services like public transport, further isolating many of the older generation.

Often, the challenge is not just to ensure that big cities cope with all the newcomers and population growth – it is also about guaranteeing a good quality of life for those left behind.

11. ACT
BUILD CITIES FOR PEOPLE. DON'T GET CARRIED AWAY WITH TECHNOLOGY

DANISH ARCHITECT JAN GEHL HAS DEVOTED MUCH OF HIS LIFE TO DESIGNING CITIES FOR PEOPLE. HE IS SCEPTICAL OF OUR OBSESSION WITH TECHNOLOGY, BELIEVING IT OVERLOOKS HUMAN NEEDS, IS TOO EXPENSIVE AND FAILS TO MAKE A DIFFERENCE WHERE IT IS NEEDED MOST

Jan Gehl delivered an explosive speech in Copenhagen recently on the subject of sustainable cities. But he could just as well have been in Jakarta, Moscow, Sao Paolo, Chicago, Beijing or any other of the world's big and rapidly growing cities. The 81-year-old Danish architect is highly sought after as an internationally acclaimed authority on designing cities that are good places to live.

Gehl insists that urban planning should be on a human scale.

"For the last half-century, we've built cities for cars, not for people," he says.

"Everything is designed to allow us to rush around at 60 miles per hour. Cities have big roads, giant billboards, long stretches devoid of life. Building on a human scale involves paying due heed to our bodies, our need for eye contact, to meet, think, speak, play and move about. Long, enclosed passages make us feel uneasy. But whenever life is within easy reach on foot or by bike, whenever we have access to inviting meeting places and public areas, small shops and so

on, then people thrive in these enjoyable and pleasant surroundings. We need places we can meander around in at three miles per hour instead of charging about at 60."

Gehl graduated in 1960. At that time, he and many of his peers were enamoured with the modernist conception of the city as a rational machine that exists to fulfil basic needs as efficiently as possible. Human beings were part of that machine and had to adapt to it.

He then married Ingrid, a behavioural psychologist, who challenged the modernist mindset in urban planning on the grounds that it failed to take account of the things that help people live well. She famously asked her new husband, "Why are you architects not interested in people?"

This marked the beginning of their shared life's work of designing cities for people, instead of the other way around. They believe cities should be friendly and vibrant places that respect the human scale and fulfil people's desire to see and do things together and spend time in each other's company.

Jan Gehl in one of the many pedestrianised streets of Copenhagen. Building a city on a human scale increases our sense of belonging and well-being, he says.

"It's something that we, as humans, already have hundreds of years of practice in. Cities built before the age of the car were on that scale," says Gehl, pointing to Copenhagen and Venice as prime examples.

When it comes to sustainable cities, Gehl believes that we are allowing ourselves to be seduced by technology all too quickly. Autonomous vehicles, transport drones and smart cities alone will not help the urban conurbations that are in the most urgent need of improvement: the rapidly growing urban centres of Asia, South America and Africa.

"Sustainability is too expensive to introduce on the requisite scale in those places. Fortunately, we also have low-tech solutions that we know work. We can plan cities so that people can get around easily on foot or by bike, complemented by a high-quality public transport system. People need to move around, but cities that are designed for cars are almost impossible to navigate on foot or by bike. This has a negative impact on our health. The medical journal *The Lancet* published a study showing that people who live in the suburbs now have a lower

life expectancy than those who live in the inner city. This is because the suburbs were built for cars, but we still do more walking and cycling in downtown areas. Cities designed for cars are expensive because they are harmful to our health in so many ways," says Gehl, citing the mayor of Bogota as someone who understands the importance of a different approach to urban planning.

His first priority is to improve mobility for the 80% who don't own cars – if they are able to get around on foot, by bike or on public transport, then they will have better job opportunities in other, wealthier parts of the city. This sector of the population derives no benefit from improved conditions for cars – or even autonomous vehicles.

"All sorts of companies are producing all sorts of smart new technology for cities that they want to seduce us into buying. But based on centuries of experience, we already know what makes a city truly sustainable – putting people first."

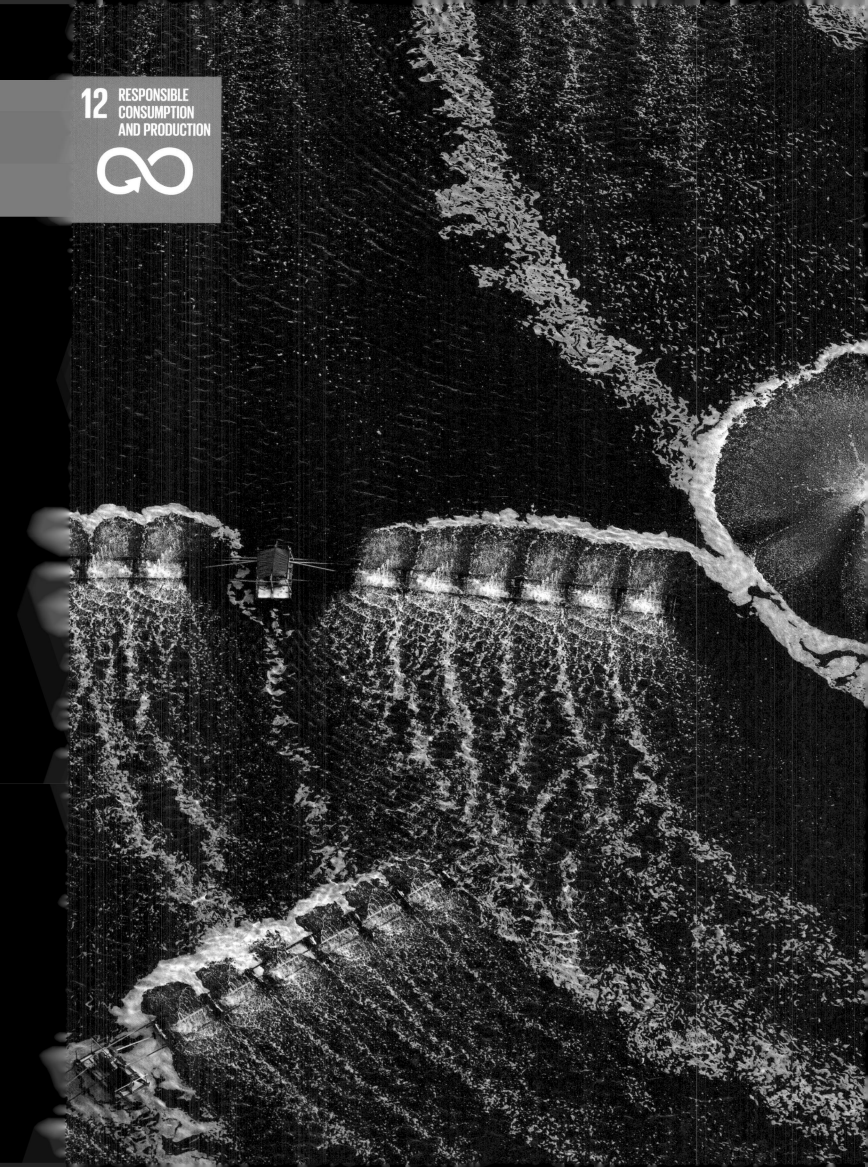

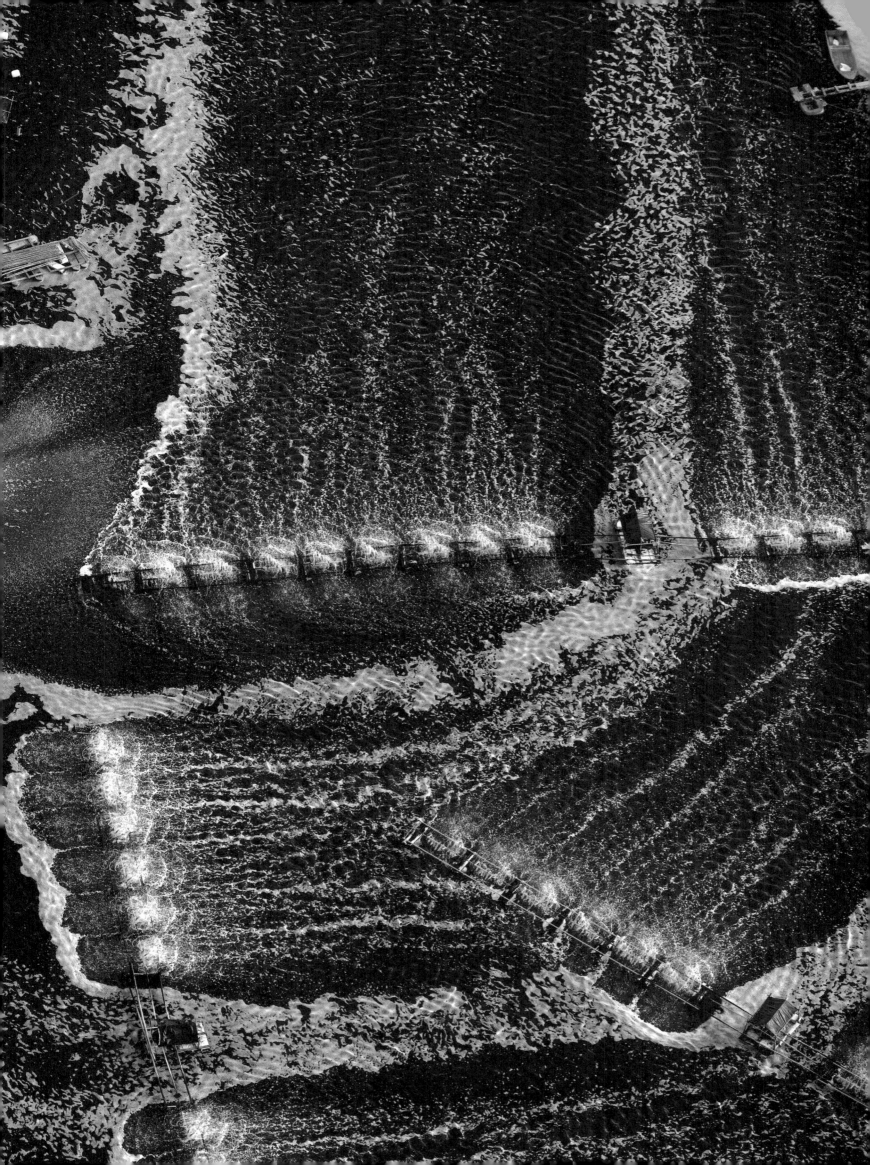

GOAL 12

- -

RESPONSIBLE CONSUMPTION AND PRODUCTION

- -

"I LOVE THE IDEA OF FINDING SOMETHING THAT IS DIFFERENT, THAT HAS A STORY AND MISSION.

I created **lemlem** and **the lemlem Foundation** with the goal of improving lives through incredible high-end fashion. We're able to affect so many people's lives through what we do. There's something really beautiful about closing the circle by creating a more sustainable business model that enables artisans to be independent. Proceeds from our direct sales are donated to the lemlem Foundation to fund maternal health and women's empowerment programmes in Africa. The consumer can be happy about buying something one-of-a-kind that has positive repercussions"

LIYA KEBEDE

Model and founder, lemlem and lemlem Foundation

Previous double page: Shrimp farm, Phang Nga Bay, Thailand
(8° 23' N – 98° 34' E)

GOAL 12
ENSURE SUSTAINABLE CONSUMPTION AND PRODUCTION PATTERNS

The vision: By 2030 we will sustainably manage and make efficient use of natural resources. Chemicals and waste products will be managed in an environmentally sound manner, and less waste will be generated. Companies, especially large and transnational enterprises, will be encouraged to adopt sustainable practices, public-procurement practices will be sustainable, and subsidies for fossil fuels will end

TRASHING THE WORLD

TOGETHER WE GENERATE
2 BILLION TONS
OF SOLID WASTE
ANNUALLY. IN 2030
THIS IS PROJECTED
TO HAVE RISEN TO
2.6 BILLION
TONS

(**Source:** World Bank:
What a Waste 2.0, 2018)

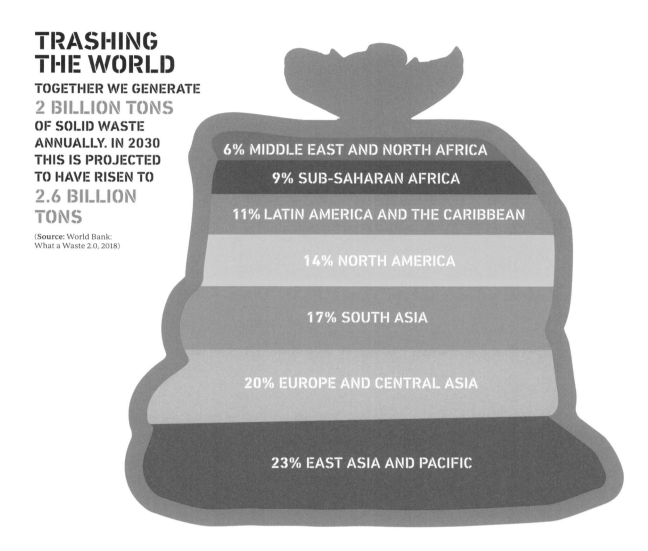

6% MIDDLE EAST AND NORTH AFRICA

9% SUB-SAHARAN AFRICA

11% LATIN AMERICA AND THE CARIBBEAN

14% NORTH AMERICA

17% SOUTH ASIA

20% EUROPE AND CENTRAL ASIA

23% EAST ASIA AND PACIFIC

WASTE NOT, WANT NOT

Based on current population and consumption trends, by 2050 it will take three years for Earth to replenish the natural resources that humans use every year. This is unsustainable. "There is no planet B", as the saying goes. This is it.

It is essential that we drastically reduce global consumption at the same time as we are working on the goals of eradicating poverty, ending hunger and ensuring a good quality of life for all. We need growth, but of a type that benefits everyone and makes responsible use of resources.

A good place to start is with what we throw away. Households alone account for a veritable mountain of waste – 2 billion tons p.a., half of which comes from the wealthiest nations.

We discard and squander vast resources – on everything from ice cream wrappers to unused old

ships. Recycling levels are currently very low, but that is changing. Denmark, for example, recycles waste and uses it as fuel in district heating systems in urban areas. This is still wasteful, but preferable to just discarding waste. Many countries are turning materials like glass and paper into new products. Unfortunately, the vast majority of our waste still ends up polluting the environment in landfill sites.

Recycling alone will not reverse the whittling away of Earth's resources. We need products made of sustainable and biodegradable materials that don't pose risks to the people who work with them and don't pollute the environment at the end of their life cycle. We need new products made of materials that are easy to separate and recycle. The first priority, however, is to be much better at rethinking and designing products so that they don't draw as heavily on finite resources – in other words, more durable products that are renewable rather than disposable.

12. CREATE
CHRISTIAN BOLTANSKI

"ALL THESE CLOTHES IN **NO MAN'S LAND** ARE DEAD CLOTHES. BUT IF SOMEBODY SAYS 'YOU ARE MINE', A NEW LIFE WILL BEGIN..."

What kind of traces do we leave behind? French artist Christian Boltanski has devoted much of his long career to exploring the question of what it means to be human. He has a particular interest in the traces we leave behind, both in life and in death.

Not so long ago, if people left anything behind, it was bequeathed to the next generation. Nowadays, overconsumption, including of clothes, generates veritable mountains of waste. Boltanski's work *No Man's Land* uses the discarded outfits of 400,000 people – 30 tons in total. Tellingly, he had no problem getting his hands on such an enormous volume of used clothing.

"There are too many clothes in the world nowadays. The man who supplied the clothes for the exhibition handles 100 tons a day and destroying it all is a huge problem. Nowadays, a lot of people don't keep their clothes. They're cheap and the quality isn't great – so people just throw them out after a couple of months. Some of it – perhaps 10% – goes to Africa. Most of it is turned into felt."

As part of the work, a crane with a giant claw dives into the pile at regular intervals, grabs a random bundle of clothes, raises it up and then lets it go to tumble down the side of the mountain once more. It is evocative of the hand of God or fate, which – seemingly without rhyme or reason – suddenly plucks us out of our everyday lives and alters our destiny.

CHRISTIAN BOLTANSKI

French sculptor, photographer, painter and film maker, most well known for his photography installations and contemporary conceptual style. **Artwork:** *Personnes (No Man's Land)*, 2010.

Boltanski's art can be interpreted in many ways, and *No Man's Land* is no exception. In French, the work is called *Personnes*, which can mean either "people" or "nobodies". The piles of used clothes contain traces of their former owners, who are now unknown and invisible and only endowed with the personalities and identities ascribed to them by the person viewing the work.

Personnes can also be understood as a comment on the copious quantities of material goods and overindulgence so prevalent in consumer society. We leave so much behind us, in life as well as in death, and this in itself reduces us to "personnes" – to anonymous consumers devoid of individual value.

12. THINK PETS OR PESTS?

AS THE GLOBAL PET INDUSTRY CONTINUES TO GROW EXPONENTIALLY, AND ANIMALS BECOME MORE AND MORE A PART OF THE FAMILY, RESEARCHERS WARN THAT THE LEVEL OF RESOURCES REQUIRED TO PROVIDE FOOD, ACCESSORIES AND HEALTH CARE FOR ALL THESE ANIMALS IS UNSUSTAINABLE

Blueberries, oats, honey and yoghurt. No, it's not the breakfast menu in a trendy city café. It's the ingredients in a face mask for dogs. If the ads are to be believed, this product will give your precious mutt a more beautiful coat, dirt-free tear ducts and an aromatherapy-induced inner calm.

After its facial, how about a canine yoga session or fitness class? Or Dog TV to while away the hours? Or some holistic treats to keep it natural and healthy? Or a crystal-studded collar to ward off the negative aspects of the modern dog's life? Toys are huge, too.

It may all sound a bit extreme, but the examples reflect a wider trend. The pet industry is one of the fastest-growing in the world. In the USA alone, turnover of $100 billion is predicted by 2020.

The picture is much the same in other Western countries, and in Asia. Nobody publishes exact statistics for the global pet population, but the USA, thought to be the greatest dog-loving nation, is home to around 90 million dogs and 94 million cats.

Some estimates put the global pet population at close to a billion, and the link between rising income and

pet ownership is pretty clear. Dogs cost the most in terms of resources. In the USA, the dogs-to-people ratio is already higher than 1:4. If the rest of the world were to follow suit, our best friends would soon reach the two billion mark.

In an era in which the depletion of resources is a major concern and overpopulation poses a serious problem, experts such as the environmental research organisation Worldwatch Institute warn that pet numbers of that magnitude would be unsustainable.

Senior researcher Erik Assadourian points out that two fully grown Alsatians consume more food than the average human in Bangladesh, and that the dog population of the USA uses more resources than the people of Haiti and Cuba combined. However, in contrast to the high levels of public and political awareness surrounding the environmental impact of cars, little attention has been paid to the booming pet industry.

Pet food manufacturers are well aware of the issue and are taking steps such as using leftovers from human food production in dog and cat food. But they are also under pressure to stand out in a fiercely competitive market, to grab the attention of pet owners. Often, they do so by advertising luxury products made with real, tender meat, which owners buy to give their beloved pets food of the same high quality as their own.

According to experts, feeding pets like this is not in their interests. And all that food has to come out again. America's dogs produce 11 million tons of excrement each year – more than the human population did in 1959. This is harmful to the environment, as are the plastic bags used by responsible dog owners.

It may be an unpopular view, but Assadourian believes that we need to reconsider our approach to keeping pets. Animals have become such an integral part of our family life that few would consider parting with them or countenance a ban. But we can take steps to reduce both the number of pets and the resources devoted to them, e.g. by imposing higher taxes on accessories.

The Worldwatch Institute also proposes the introduction of compulsory sterilisation and castration (except for professional breeders) to keep the number of cats and dogs down. Another option would be to return to keeping pets that are useful, e.g. hens, goats and rabbits, which are edible.

Pet-sharing schemes are also an option. Assadourian notes that our attachment to pets is sometimes indicative of loneliness and a yearning for company. He argues that stronger social networks and more lively local communities could help to fulfil many of the human needs currently met by pets.

The late Sir David Mackay, climate change adviser, physicist and mathematician, offered some simple advice: buy pets the same way you buy cars – few and small.

PALM OIL IS BAD, THE ALTERNATIVES WORSE

We've all seen images of imperilled orang-utans fleeing from burning rainforests, as giant machines crush and destroy their habitat to clear a path for one of the most valuable crops in the world – palm oil.

According to the International Union for Conservation of Nature (IUCN), 193 endangered and vulnerable species, including tigers and gibbons, are directly threatened as oil palm trees supplant indigenous forests and destroy the habitats of innumerable species. Oil palm plantations have eradicated half of Borneo's orang-utan population in less than two decades.

The way palm oil is cultivated at the moment is quite simply unsustainable. Despite agreeing to protect indigenous forests and take into account the needs of local populations, many companies continue to harvest palm oil illegally and in breach of their promises.

Large numbers of consumers and grassroots movements have called for a complete boycott of the product, and advocate the use of rapeseed, sunflower or other forms of vegetable oil. But those solutions are potentially even less sustainable. An IUCN report into the impact of palm oil and of replacing it with other plant oils warns that deforestation and the damage to diversity is likely to be exacerbated by a boycott of palm oil, rather than slowed down.

It's quite simple, really – oil palm trees have by far the highest yield per acre. Replacing palm oil with soy, sunflower or rapeseed oil would require significantly more land – in many cases, up to nine times as much. Production companies would have to fell vast swathes of tropical rainforest or savannah in South America and Africa.

The IUCN would prefer governments and companies to introduce regulation and monitoring and guarantee sustainable palm oil production. Environmental organisations such as Greenpeace – which campaigns against "dirty palm oil" – and the World Wide Fund for Nature also back the campaign for a certification scheme to guarantee more sustainable production. According to the IUCN, palm oil from certified plantations is at present only marginally more sustainable than non-certified oil. However, the scheme has considerable potential to increase sustainability in the industry if fully adapted.

12. ACT
CÉLINE COUSTEAU: SHARE WHAT YOU KNOW AND INSPIRE OTHERS

"The people of the Vale do Javari taught me a lot about their lives and in turn I learned a lot more about myself, and about having a vision further into the future," says **Céline Cousteau.**

"PEOPLE PROTECT WHAT THEY LOVE"

CÉLINE COUSTEAU, EXPLORER AND ENVIRONMENTAL CAMPAIGNER

Céline first set foot in the Amazon when she was nine, on an expedition led by her grandfather, Jacques Cousteau. In a forest teeming with life, they encountered multiple tribes living as they had done since time immemorial. A quarter of a century later, she was on her way back to the Amazon, this time with her father and brother. The task of engaging with the tribes, including in Peru, had now fallen to her.

"I naïvely thought they'd be pleased to see us. But the chief didn't pull his punches: "What will you being here do for us?"

Céline began to explain how it would be good for the tribe to raise awareness of its predicament so others would understand. The chief just shook his head.

"Let me tell you something. Doctors from all over the world come here to learn from our shamans and healers. So do anthropologists wanting to learn about our history and traditions. They all say that they'll help us with the attacks on our land and people, but as soon as their studies are published or their pills available, we never hear from them again. You say that you'll show the world the challenges we're facing and how we struggle. But then what? They will have seen this and maybe felt sorry for us, but nothing will happen."

Right there and then, Céline understood that documentation isn't enough. "You have to ask people what they need," she says, "and provide opportunities for action."

It is a realisation that has driven her work ever since, and she always keeps her grandfather's words in the back of her mind: "People protect what they love, they love what they understand, and they understand what they are taught."

"My grandfather started off as an explorer, but he changed as he learned and understood. He realised that we need to protect and conserve. I see this as an essential part of my own mission in life: to share knowledge and potential courses of action."

Given her family legacy, it was almost inevitable that Céline would follow in the footsteps of her grandparents and parents to become involved in nature conservation. Her father, Jean-Michel, is an environmental activist. Her mother, Anne-Marie, was an expedition photographer, while her brother, Fabien, is an ocean explorer and activist. Her cousins Philippe and Alexandra Cousteau, have also followed suit.

Not that there was ever any pressure or expectation that she would follow in their footsteps, she emphasizes.

"While in high school, we lived in an old brownstone building in New York. To get to the apartment, I had to go through my parents' office. My mother, who was an expedition photographer and a photo librarian, would be there sifting through thousands of slides from the field expeditions. I was immersed in this life. I couldn't help but share my family's values and understanding," she says.

"Through their work and all of the stories that they brought back, I came to understand how we are all connected to so many places. I believe that we are all part of a global energy, a spirituality, and that thi is in part our mutual connection with this planet. We need a shift in consciousness to make us more aware of our interconnectedness with each other and with nature," she says.

Through her film and impact campaign, Tribes on the Edge, Céline is working indigenous peoples of the Vale do Javari in the Brazilian Amazon. Although Indigenous Peoples account for just 4% of the world's population, the fact that they live in some of the richest ecosystems on Earth means that they are stewards of around 80% of all biodiversity. As an activist working in various fields, Céline also promotes greater sustainability and responsible consumption, including through her collaborations with corporations, foundations, individuals, and NGOs .

"Most people want to do something, but many feel overwhelmed. They see these gigantic problems and feel powerless to do anything about them. But they aren't. That's why it's so important to provide opportunities for action. Every little bit helps - each positive action is a shift towards a greater connection and perhaps even, deeper consciousness."

CÉLINE COUSTEAU'S ADVICE ON BEING A RESPONSIBLE CONSUMER

• If you've learned something that makes a difference, or something important, **SHARE IT**. Inspire your friends, family and social circle.

• To protect the ocean and large swathes of the land, avoid single-use plastic such as cutlery, straws and cups. Alternatives abound – e.g. bamboo and metal straws. **SUPPORT** others who are trying to be sustainable.

• If you do eat fish, eat only fish caught sustainably, and avoid species threatened with extinction. Overfishing has pushed many species to the brink. **USE** one of the free apps designed to help, e.g. Sustainable Seafood Guide and Seafood Watch.

• Support organisations that fight for what you believe in. Of course you can donate– but your time is also valuable – maybe you're good at bookkeeping or something else practical. The **HELP** you give to the organisation helps the cause.

• If you know about environmental or humanitarian issues, volunteer to share what you know with local schools. Education is key! Everybody capable of it should **PASS ON** what they know.

• **VOLUNTEER** in your local community – building homes, helping out at food banks – so much needs done.

GOAL 13

CLIMATE ACTION

"WE NEED POSITIVE ACTION AS FAST AS POSSIBLE.

Climate change and human rights are inextricably linked. The challenges to achieving human dignity for all have been increased exponentially by climate change. This global issue is of particular concern to me because it directly affects human rights. If we don't tackle climate change now, our efforts to improve people's everyday lives will be to no avail. What we need right now is positive action and change in behaviour – and as fast as possible"

BIANCA JAGGER
Founder and President of the Bianca Jagger Human Rights Foundation

Previous double page: Icebergs and Adelie penguins, Adelie Land, Antarctica (South Pole)
(66° 00' S – 141° 00' E)

GOAL 13
TAKE URGENT ACTION TO COMBAT CLIMATE CHANGE AND ITS IMPACTS

The vision: By 2030 we will have better and stronger capacity to handle climate-related hazards and natural disasters in all countries. Climate change measures will be integrated into national policies, strategies and planning, and all countries will be aware of climate change mitigation, adaptation, impact reduction and early warnings. Developed countries will provide financial assistance to developing countries to enhance their capacity for mitigating climate change, and to ensure effective planning in the least developed countries and small island developing states

THE INVISIBLE POLLUTION

HEATING, ELECTRICITY AND FARMING ARE RESPONSIBLE FOR NEARLY HALF THE WORLD'S GREENHOUSE GAS EMISSIONS

(**Source:** IPCC: EXIT based on global emissions from 2010)

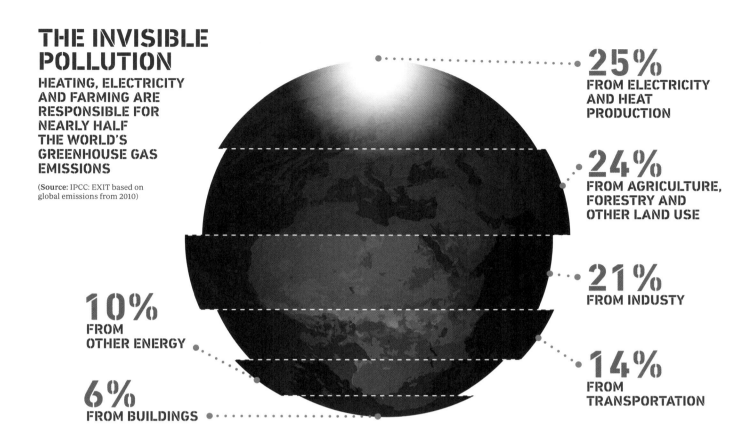

25%
FROM ELECTRICITY AND HEAT PRODUCTION

24%
FROM AGRICULTURE, FORESTRY AND OTHER LAND USE

21%
FROM INDUSTY

14%
FROM TRANSPORTATION

10%
FROM OTHER ENERGY

6%
FROM BUILDINGS

CREATOR AND DESTROYER OF CIVILISATIONS

For at least 90% of human evolutionary history, we were hunter-gatherers. We lived in scattered tribes and much of our waking time was devoted to gathering and preparing food or making tools to help us do so.

Around 12,000 years ago, a massive shift took place: Earth's climate became more stable. An era of rapid and relentless change gave way to more predictable seasons. Across vast swathes of land, temperatures and precipitation stabilised at levels that allowed humans to cultivate crops.

This change was crucial to the emergence of modern civilisation. Our ancestors started to settle in one place and cultivate the land. They domesticated animals as beasts of burden or as sources of food and clothing, from milk and meat to wool and hides. This new farming culture meant more regular food supplies, and in turn freed up time and energy to devote to the development of what we now call civilisation.

History shows that drastic climate changes not only give birth to civilisations but also bring about their

downfall. Drought and floods have wiped whole civilisations from the map, leaving only ruins to tell their story. The temple complex of Angkor Wat in Cambodia, part of the Khmer Empire, for example, was the largest and most complex city of the pre-industrial era, but it was devastated by prolonged drought.

Whenever change occurs slowly, people and nature have time to adapt. The pace and unstable nature of climate change in the 21st century pose multiple challenges. It is difficult to adapt unless you can predict what you need to adapt to.

The wealthiest countries may have the money to ameliorate some of the worst extremes of climate change, but other parts of the world are less privileged. Their populations have only two options: live with the consequences – or flee from them. Millions have already taken flight, leading to competition for already limited resources in neighbouring areas and countries. Drastic climate change aggravates other threats to peace, human rights, health and welfare. The climate is, after all, one of the basic pillars of human civilisation.

13. CREATE
OLAFUR ELIASSON

"I BELIEVE THAT ART AND CULTURE HAVE AN IMPORTANT ROLE TO PLAY IN THE EMOTIONAL CONTEXTUALISATION OF RAW FACTS AND FIGURES, AND THUS IN MOTIVATING PEOPLE TO TAKE THAT STEP FROM THOUGHT TO ACTION"

OLAFUR ELIASSON

Danish-Icelandic artist, merging science and art, exploring climate, weather and other forces of nature in his large-scale installations employing elements such as light, water, and air temperature. **Artworks:** *The weather project*, 2003. Next page: *Ice Watch*, 2015, in collaboration with Minik Rosing.

In late 2015, in the run-up to the big COP 21 climate conference in Paris, 12 gigantic ice blocks were arranged in a circle, resembling a clock face, on the Place du Panthéon in the heart of the French capital.

The blocks had sheared off from a glacier and were hauled out of Nuup Kangerlua Fjord, outside Nuuk in Greenland. Olafur Eliasson's *Ice Watch* served as a sharp reminder, both to the people of Paris and to the world leaders at the summit, of the urgent need to put the brakes on global warming. Walking in or around the ice clock – a co-production by the Danish-Icelandic artist and Minik Rosing, a Greenlandic professor of geology – people could see, hear and feel the ice melting.

The Greenland ice sheet is more than three kilometres high at its thickest point. If it were to melt completely, it would cause the sea level to rise by more than six metres, with disastrous consequences for vast swathes of the human population.

Most people find it difficult to relate to abstract figures, but Eliasson's blocks of ice were tangible and immediate, which is typical of his *modus operandi*. He engages the audience in direct physical experiences that make them feel, hear and see things in a new way. Eliasson tends to work on a large scale, and often incorporates elements of weather and landscape into his work, which is profoundly influenced by

the dramatic nature of his native Iceland, with its suddenly shifting light, wind and precipitation. As the name suggests, nature was definitely at the heart of *The weather project* at the Tate Modern in London. Visitors were greeted by a giant sun and a fine mist – as if the weather had accompanied them inside.

He is deeply concerned by climate change and by the staggering inequality that still leaves more than one billion people without access to electricity. This was the reality that inspired the solar energy project "Little Sun", which seeks to bring clean light, one lamp at a time, to places without access to an electricity grid.

13. THINK
GRAVE DANGER HERALDS
OPPORTUNITIES

ON THE ONE HAND, CLIMATE CHANGE POSES A SERIOUS THREAT TO THE MAJOR GLOBAL HEALTH ACHIEVEMENTS OF THE PAST 50 YEARS. ON THE OTHER, INTERNATIONAL EXPERTS BELIEVE THAT POTENTIAL MEASURES TO COMBAT CLIMATE CHANGE ALSO OFFER UNPARALLELED OPPORTUNITIES TO IMPROVE HEALTH OUTCOMES FOR ALL

First, the bad news: rising temperatures and an unpredictable climate pose a serious threat to the health of billions. Storms, droughts, floods and heatwaves may be nothing new, but they are set to become more frequent and ferocious – and countless more people will suffer.

The consequences are already plain to see. 2018 saw extreme heatwaves engulf large swathes of the planet, killing thousands of people. While droughts increase the risk of hunger and malnutrition, floods and violent storms destroy lives, land and livelihoods. Climate change stands to have an unparalleled impact on our lives – so much so that all of the great health advances of the past 50 years could be turned on their head, experts warn.

Plenty of column inches have been devoted to this, but less attention has been paid to the fact that the same experts also believe that climate change affords us the greatest opportunity in more than a century to raise the standard of global health.

Nick Watts is a medical doctor and head of the Lancet Countdown on Health and Climate Change – a global partnership of health experts that is monitoring trends in the run-up to 2030 and lobbying global leaders to take action to combat climate change by addressing the threats head-on and reaping the rewards. According to Watts, there are many benefits.

"Human health and the environment are closely linked. We've known this for a long time, but in recent decades we've lost sight of it, as health has increasingly been turned into a question of individual responsibility. However, the action required to halt climate change will also result in fewer premature deaths, higher life expectancy, and healthier diets – to name just a few of the advantages," he explains.

In Dhaka, Bangladesh, and in many other cities, a mixture of burning waste, traffic pollution and cooking stoves adds up to a life-threatening smog.

"IF 8 MILLION PEOPLE A YEAR WERE DYING AS A RESULT OF SOMETHING WE WERE PUTTING IN THE WATER, THERE WOULD PROBABLY BE AN OUTCRY"

The biggest benefit would be ending the world's reliance on fossil fuels. According to the WHO, approximately 8 million premature deaths p.a. are attributable to air pollution, mainly from transport and power stations. Cleaner air could lead to a significant reduction in instances of asthma, cardiovascular disorders and some forms of cancer. Recent research also indicates that air pollution plays a role in obesity and diabetes, while noise pollution from transport poses a serious health threat, in the form of stress.

However, aside from the smog that envelops some of the biggest cities, pollution is largely an invisible problem. We don't see "air pollution" or "noise" cited on death certificates. This means that the direct link between our poisoning of the environment and the countless deaths it causes remains unacknowledged in the media and public consciousness.

"If 8 million people a year were dying as a result of something we were putting in the water, there would probably be an outcry," Watts points out.

In the world's poorest countries, indoor air pollution is the most serious problem. Food is prepared over an open fire or on inefficient coal-burning stoves, which require large amounts of charcoal and exacerbate climate change due to deforestation.

Addressing air pollution is just one example of how fighting climate change goes hand in hand with improving health. Similarly, cycling or walking instead of driving not only reduces pollution but are also important forms of exercise. Scientists are increasingly aware that inactive lifestyles are just as dangerous as smoking.

Another main cause of climate change is meat consumption, primarily in the wealthier parts of the world.

"A lot of people could do with cutting down on how much meat they eat. If we want to reduce the risk of things like bowel cancer, our diet should predominantly consist of plant-based foods. We're only just beginning to understand how the bacteria in our digestive systems affect our health, but research suggests that a rich bacterial culture is vital, and this appears to be enhanced by plant-based foods."

There are other, more subtle benefits, too. For example, it has been documented that rising temperatures lead to a fall in productivity, particularly in tropical areas. Understandably, there is a limit to how much work can be done in extremely hot conditions, which leads to poverty and in turn exacerbates the risk of malnutrition and ill health.

Using cleaner indoor energy sources and generating electricity from solar and wind power also have positive effects other than just reducing deforestation and deaths caused by air pollution. More efficient stoves allow for faster cooking, leaving more free time to work or run a business. This benefits women in particular, enhancing both economic prosperity and gender equality.

A healthier environment and a flourishing natural world mean improved food safety and a reduced risk of some of the infectious diseases that originate in wildlife, such as bird flu and Ebola. When nature is depleted, humans and domestic animals are at greater risk of coming into contact with infected animals – a situation that can quickly escalate into a deadly epidemic.

Many of the proposed measures are what Watts terms "no regrets" solutions – regardless of the effect on climate change, there is nothing to lose by introducing them. Less air pollution, greater food security, reduced meat consumption, more exercise, greener cities, richer nature – these are outcomes that are beneficial to all. They will save millions from premature death and alleviate the suffering of many more.

"We know what needs to be done, but there is a lack of political will," says Watts. He adds that those in positions of power would do well to heed the principles of cardiac massage: "push hard, push fast, don't stop". The pressure we apply to halt climate change needs to be hard, fast and persistent.

COOL IT!

Keeping cool poses a massive threat to the climate. About one-fifth of all electricity is used on refrigeration and air conditioning. To compound matters, the gases pumped into refrigeration systems are 1,000 to 9,000 times more harmful to the climate than CO_2.

Houses, food and medicine all need to be kept cool. Too much food is wasted because it isn't chilled properly, particularly in developing countries. As the climate heats up, the number of people who will need cooling units will rise, and greater global prosperity will mean they are able to afford refrigerators and air conditioning. It is more urgent than ever to find environmentally friendly ways of keeping cool.

One important climate project, "Drawdown", looked at various ways of slowing climate change. It concluded that the single most effective solution would be better refrigeration and air-conditioning systems.

The political commitment to phasing out harmful gases from refrigeration units already exists, in the form of the 2016 Kigali Agreement. The wealthiest countries agreed to start phasing out harmful gases straight away while developing countries were given ten years' grace.

Natural replacements are already available but don't solve the problem of the 3 billion or so fridges and air-conditioning units that are already out there. It is when fridges are scrapped that they release harmful gases. Capturing and storing these gases is expensive and difficult – but also vital.

Kigali was, without doubt, a significant step in the right direction, but cooling systems still pose a huge and immediate challenge, not least because they use staggering amounts of electricity. Another challenge is to come up with cooling methods that work in places with no electricity, or where people are too poor to pay for them.

Ancient techniques have a role to play – using ventilation, shade and materials to build homes that keep cool naturally. Planting trees near houses and along streets helps keep temperatures down and provide valuable shade. Simple jar systems – a layer of wet sand between two earthenware jars – can keep food cool for days, just as well as any fridge. This method is particularly widespread in Africa.

At the other end of the scale, researchers and companies all over the world are competing to come up with efficient new systems that use less energy and cut out the harmful gases.

Sure Chill, one of the most promising new technologies, harnesses a unique property of water – i.e. that it is at its most dense at precisely 4°C but expands and rises at any other temperature. This is why ice rises to the top of a lake while fish swim around below the surface. Crucially, 4°C also happens to be the ideal temperature at which to store food, drink and life-saving vaccines. Sure Chill has produced a water-based refrigeration system that maintains a steady temperature of 4° for up to ten days without electricity. The UN already uses it to store vaccines in areas with no electricity, and the technology has the potential to be radically transformative.

SAIL IS BACK

Shipping is far and away the most effective and environmentally friendly way to transport large quantities of goods. Unfortunately, it also uses huge amounts of fuel, often of the least environmentally friendly kind.

In 2018, the 174 nations that make up the International Maritime Organisation (IMO) agreed to halve emissions from shipping by 2050 – a target that will demand a radical new approach. Potential solutions range from more efficient shipbuilding and new types of fuel to solar-powered vessels and very slow ships (known as slow-steaming ships) with minimal fuel consumption.

Another solution would be to bring back sail, albeit of a new type. Rotor sails are giant cylinders that look like chimneys. They are based on the Magnus effect – the wind causes the cylindrical sails to rotate, which propels the ship forward. The German engineer Anton Flettner first used this technology on a ship in 1926. At the time, fuel was cheap and readily available, and his innovative thinking attracted little interest. Now, times have changed. New, improved and lighter materials have brought rotor sails back into the mix and piqued the interest of shipping companies, including the huge Danish company Maersk, which is experimenting with the technology.

13. ACT
THAI MOTHER PUTS HER LIFE ON THE LINE

JINTANA KAEWKAO FIGHTS AGAINST THE DESTRUCTION OF THAILAND'S CLIMATE AND ENVIRONMENT

In 2017, four people per week were murdered somewhere in the world for protesting against the destruction of the environment or the loss of land rights, according to Global Witness, which exposes corruption and attacks on environmentalists. Such attacks are relatively common in Thailand. Jintana Kaewkao knows this all too well, as she found her life turned upside down when she led local resistance to a coal-fired power plant more than two decades ago.

The power station would have stopped the people of the town being able to fish from their local beach. The management promised good jobs and a financial boost for the community. However, Kaewkao and others argued that the overall impact would be negative, and it shouldn't be built.

The campaign set Kaewkao on the path to becoming one of the best-known activists in Thailand. Previously, she spent her days looking after her three children and running a small grocery store. Suddenly, she was at the forefront of a movement.

In 2001, Kaewkao was shot at for the first time, by an unknown gunman. She has since survived other attempts on her life and has been imprisoned several times.

Kaewkao says that when she started the protests, she didn't know very much about climate change. At the time, her focus was on protecting nature and life in her village. However, when she learned about coal-fired power stations and the role they play in climate change, she and the other campaigners were able to bring new arguments to bear. It took a few years, but ultimately the villagers won. The beach and nature in the area may have been saved, but Kaewkao is still active whenever Thailand's environment is under threat.

"It's not enough to talk about climate change, to just put on a badge," she says. "We all have to act."

Jintana Kaewkao holds a meeting of villagers at her home. She is one of Thailand's best known environmental activists and has survived several attempted murders.

GOAL 14

- -

LIFE BELOW WATER

- -

"SOME HAVE CALLED THE OCEAN THE WORLD'S BIGGEST BUSINESS. IF IT WERE A COUNTRY, IT WOULD BE OUR 7TH LARGEST ECONOMY.

The ocean gives us half the oxygen we breathe and absorbs a quarter of our CO_2 emissions. Its riches support the livelihoods of over 3 billion people around the world. No question, the ocean is our planetary insurance policy. But this insurance policy is at risk. Greed, short-term thinking and corruption have created a vicious cycle that threatens to tip the balance of life in the ocean and, consequently, on our beautiful planet. So, what can we do? First of all, protection is critical. Experts agree that we must protect 30% of the ocean by 2030. This will prevent fisheries from collapse, maintain biodiversity, protect livelihoods and secure food supplies. We also need leadership for the ocean, in governments as much as in business and civil society. We must not allow the ocean's tragic demise to happen right before our eyes – aided and abetted by our inaction. That is not the legacy I want to leave to my grandchildren. Business has a critical role to play – in words and actions. As captains of industry, we must also be stewards of the ocean. Those things should go hand in hand"

SIR RICHARD BRANSON

Businessman and investor, best known as the founder of Virgin Group

Previous double page: Humpback whale off Port-Gentil, Gulf of Guinea, Ogooué-Maritime province, Gabon
(0° 31' S – 8° 52' E)

GOAL 14
CONSERVE AND SUSTAINABLY USE THE OCEANS, SEAS AND MARINE RESOURCES FOR SUSTAINABLE DEVELOPMENT

The vision: By 2030 all kinds of marine pollution will have been significantly reduced. Marine and coastal ecosystems will be sustainably managed, and action will be taken to restore them, in order to ensure healthy and productive oceans. Enhanced scientific cooperation will help address the impacts of ocean acidification. Overfishing will be a thing of the past, as will illegal, unreported and unregulated fishing, and other destructive practices. At least 10% of coastal and marine areas will be conservation areas

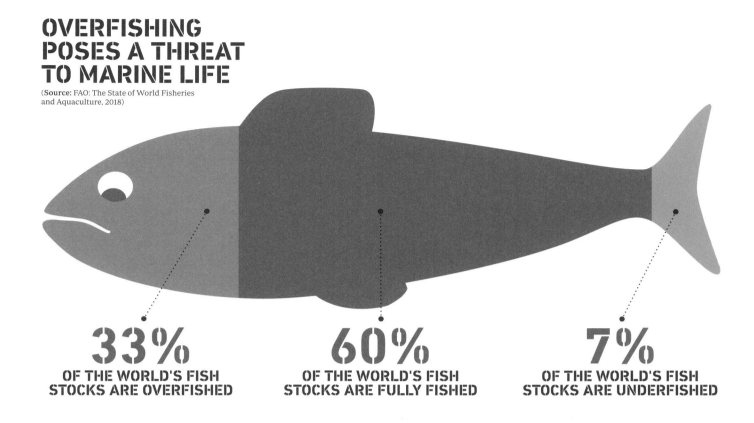

OVERFISHING POSES A THREAT TO MARINE LIFE

(**Source:** FAO: The State of World Fisheries and Aquaculture, 2018)

33% OF THE WORLD'S FISH STOCKS ARE OVERFISHED

60% OF THE WORLD'S FISH STOCKS ARE FULLY FISHED

7% OF THE WORLD'S FISH STOCKS ARE UNDERFISHED

THE SEAS CAN'T WAIT!

All life came from the sea. The Danish author Karen Blixen famously wrote, "I know of a cure for everything: salt water… in one way or the other. Sweat, or tears, or the salt sea."

It is true that the seas help to sustain approximately half the world's population. They are our single biggest source of protein and home to our richest eco-systems. They cover almost three-quarters of the Earth's surface – and vast areas of ocean remain unexplored.

The seas contain riches that even a few decades ago seemed inexhaustible – but that was an illusion. At least 90% of fish stocks are now either overfished and on the verge of collapse or exploited to the limit. Fertilisers, heavy metals and toxins seep from our coasts out into the sea, creating dead zones. Plastic pollutes huge areas.

Rising temperatures are killing coral reefs, and the oceans are absorbing so much CO_2 from the atmosphere that they have become acidified, further exacerbating the destruction of marine ecosystems. Melting ice from glaciers and the poles is altering the salt balance, which inflicts great damage on currents and fish stocks.

The oceans need urgent help. We need to bring illegal fishing under control and create protection zones, safe marine breeding grounds for stocks to replenish. The oceans can't wait until 2030 – we need to act now.

Many of the tools are already available. Several countries have already intervened and are striking up international partnerships. The marine protection zones set up by some countries demonstrate how big a difference even small changes make. The narrow Sound between Denmark and Sweden flows through a densely populated area and is one of the busiest stretches of water in the world. Despite this, a long-standing ban on trawling means that a wide range of species flourish there.

It is possible to protect the oceans of the world from overfishing and protect the livelihoods of the millions of people whose income depends on fishing at the same time. But it will require extensive international co-operation and targeted and urgent action.

14. CREATE
DOUG AITKEN

"TO BRING SOMEONE INTO THE OCEAN ITSELF, TO OPEN THEM UP TO THIS SPACE AND THIS SERIES OF ENCOUNTERS, FOR ME THAT'S THE ACTIVISM"

Doug Aitken still lives close to where he grew up, on the coast of Southern California. Despite spending so much of his life next to the ocean, it was only relatively recently that the American artist came up with the idea for an artwork that would serve as a gateway to the underwater world.

Aitken's works have revolved around the themes of exploration and travel, perception and space. In *Underwater Pavilions*, he has created a work of art that audiences are invited to enter and explore, but which also confronts them with the vulnerability of the sea.

The work consists of three mirrored, geometric sculptures that are lowered into the water for visitors to swim or dive into. Beneath the surface, visitors find themselves in a kaleidoscopic observatory room, surrounded by glittering reflections of themselves and their surroundings. They are encouraged to be aware of themselves in the ocean around them, both as part of the artwork and as an alien element.

Underwater Pavilions is a portable artwork. Its first setting was the island of Catalina, off the coast of California. Next, it will move to tropical waters as part of the collaboration with Parley for the Oceans, an activist organisation that seeks to protect marine life and helped ensure that the installation had no negative impact on the marine environment.

DOUG AITKEN

American artist widely known for his innovative fine art installations. Utilising a wide array of artistic approaches, Aitken's works lead the audience into a world where time, space, and memory are fluid concepts. **Artwork:** *Underwater Pavilions*, 2016.

In California, it quickly became apparent that the opposite was, in fact, the case – the textured surfaces made an attractive habitat for a multitude of plants and creatures, bringing the sculpture to life and changing it constantly.

Aitken is increasingly driven to create art that becomes one with nature and changes with it. *Underwater Pavilions* has raised awareness of the ocean and opened the door to a new world and a way to explore it.

14. THINK
TURNING THE TIDE

WE KNOW THE PROBLEMS, WE HAVE THE SOLUTIONS. LIMITING
SINGLE-USE PLASTIC, MARINE RESERVES AND SURVEILLANCE
OF ILLEGAL FISHING ARE AMONG THE WAYS TO PROTECT
AND ENRICH MARINE LIFE

THE CONSTANT FLOOD OF PLASTIC INTO THE OCEANS

Every second of every day, about a million plastic bags are in use somewhere in the world. The UN estimates that we throw them away just 12–15 minutes later on average. Some countries recycle them. In Denmark, they are collected and used to help fuel district heating systems.

The global picture is less rosy. Bags account for 86% of all of the plastic not recycled, and much of it makes its way into the seas and poses a serious threat to marine life. Most of us have heard of "the Great Pacific Garbage Patch"– a gigantic plastic island in the Pacific Ocean more than three times the size of France – but it is by no means the only plastic litter in our seas. Every year, 13 million tons of plastic end up as marine litter, the equivalent of dumping an entire truckload of plastic waste offshore every minute.

All of this plastic pollutes the habitats of fish and seabirds and destroys huge swathes of coastline as it washes ashore. According to a McKinsey report, more than half of the waste comes from five countries: China, Indonesia, the Philippines, Thailand and Vietnam. Although it would make a massive difference if these five were to cut their waste, the problem is still a global one.

As things stand, the solution is not to eschew plastic altogether. It has many advantages: plastic cars are lighter and use less fuel, and plastic packaging preserves food for longer and helps cut food waste. What we can all do is not use plastic bags once then throw them away, buy reusable bottles, containers and boxes, use shopping bags made of recycled fibre and make sure that any plastic we can't avoid using is recycled and doesn't end up polluting the natural environment.

All around the world, projects and initiatives are attempting to rid seas and coastlines of plastic – but it will all be for naught if we fail to reduce the constant flood of the material that we pump into the oceans in the first place.

THE IMPORTANCE OF COASTAL FORESTS

The coast at Da Loc in Vietnam was once covered in mangrove forest, but it was cleared bit by bit. The local people needed wood for cooking, and the forest was in the way of the seagrasses they used for weaving mats and baskets.

Other areas were cleared to make way for shrimp farms. By now, the coasts were no longer protected by the forests, which used to prevent flooding after storms. Nothing was left to stop salt water pouring into fields and ruining crops. The land was barren for years, and large numbers of locals were forced to move away. Fish disappeared too. Inshore fishermen now had to sail for days to find the same amount of fish.

Dams built to cope with the relentless floods wore out over the years and collapsed completely when a particularly violent typhoon hit the area in 2005, devastating 250 hectares of land. The damage was incalculable, but one area was spared, the one where the mangrove forest hadn't been cleared. The dam remained intact there, and the fields survived unscathed. The mangroves took the brunt of the storm, dissipating the force of it before the waves struck land.

These events signalled the start of major local efforts to replant mangrove, in collaboration with the humanitarian organisation CARE. The forest now extends way out into the water, the fish are back, and the local people make extra income by selling the highly popular mangrove honey and from oyster and mussel fishing. Evaluations of the project estimate that every dollar spent on planting mangrove has saved $186 in money that would have been spent on flood damage.

Over half of the mangrove forests in the world have been felled, with catastrophic consequences for coastal communities. The forests serve as nurseries for a wide variety of species. When the forests disappear, so do these species. Fortunately, awareness of the benefits of replanting is now spreading around the world.

The International Union for Conservation of Nature (IUCN) points out that replanting mangrove forests addresses several of the UN 2030 Goals. Not only do the forests support marine life, but they also help the locals earn money and put food on their tables, they help to mitigate against the effects of climate change – especially by absorbing CO_2 – and they boost biodiversity in the seas and along coasts.

NEW TECHNOLOGY PROTECTS MARINE LIFE

Where do the giant trawlers actually fish? Where are the small fishing boats? What methods do they use? Until very recently, questions like these were extremely difficult to answer, but this is now changing thanks to advanced new satellites and data from the sensors now installed on most ships.

This technology could prove crucial in the fight to protect marine species and environments. More and more countries are working together on marine conservation areas, but these only make a difference if they are respected. Before digital technology, it was impossible to monitor whether this was the case. Knowledge of fishing patterns is useful when setting up conservation areas. It provides insight into the impact the efforts will have on fishing and communities.

Data acquisition and satellite surveillance are also becoming more efficient all of the time. An ever-increasing swarm of nano-satellites – usually about the size of a shoe box, and weighing 1–10 kg – take high-quality photos so frequently that we can see, almost in real time, whenever a fishing vessel enters a conservation area, coral reefs are damaged, or the ocean is polluted.

Drone surveillance is already a reality in some coastal regions. Used correctly, all of this new technology will prove valuable in protecting marine life.

14. ACT
ANDREA MARSHALL:
WE HAVE FAR MORE
POWER THAN WE REALISE

Andrea Marshall, also known as Queen of the Mantas,
swimming alongside a giant manta ray off the island of
San Benedicto, Mexico.

"MARINE LIFE IS NOW WORTH MORE ALIVE THAN IT IS CAUGHT"

ANDREA MARSHALL,
MARINE BIOLOGIST

The sand dunes are drifting. Further inland, tall palm trees stand watch, but out here on the coast, few plants thrive in the dry sand and salty wind. No urban light pollution interferes with the southern night sky and its dazzling array of stars, which seem close enough to reach out and touch.

The view by day is equally magnificent. Humpback whales swim very close to the shore and are clearly visible from the dunes as they slam their tails into the water or perform great, twisting backflips. Foam and bubbles, lighter than the surrounding water, mark the spots where they crash back into the ocean. The locals call these "blue footprints".

The waters between Mozambique and the big island of Madagascar are teeming with life, in particular with an unusually high number of the ocean's biggest creatures – from humpbacks and whale sharks to manta rays. The waters here act as a beauty parlour, with vast shoals of fish grooming their giant cousins by scouring them free of parasites.

It is her fascination with the manta ray that has led marine biologist and researcher Andrea Marshall to call the small coastal town of Barra home for the past 15 years. Her affinity with the giant fish has earned her the nickname "Queen of Mantas" – and the fledgling NGO

that she co-founded along this coast has now grown into the Marine Megafauna Foundation, which campaigns to save these ocean giants from extinction globally.

Offered positions by several world leading universities and other respected non-profits, Marshall has opted to stay in Mozambique in the family home she has built there – the third so far.

She has devoted her life to studying these giants and has greatly increased our understanding of them, even though they remain a source of great mystery.

"My work absolutely necessitates that I live in the field, so that I can monitor the populations closely, understand the behaviour and lifestyle of the animals and determine exactly what threats they face and how to curb them," Marshall explains.

Over the past 15 years, she and her team have worked tirelessly with the local people, sharing the results of their work and slowly changing attitudes towards fishing and marine conservation.

"These are places where people have always fished and where the population is entirely dependent on the income generated from the sea. You can't just barge in and tell them to stop."

In some waters off the coast of Mozambique, stocks are so depleted, and people are still so dependent on fishing, that mosquito nets are used just to make sure something is caught. It's a vicious circle, and difficult to break, but attitudes have changed here thanks to the incredible populations of whale sharks and manta rays. Barra has swiftly gained a newfound popularity as a place to dive or snorkel with these iconic marine creatures.

"Marine life is now worth more alive than it is caught," says Marshall. "Tourists provide a source of both direct and indirect income, making the local people far less dependent on fishing. Nowadays, if anybody asks whether they ever catch sharks or turtles, they look absolutely shocked. 'Of course not – we make our living from them.' It represents a momentous shift in attitude and proves that it is possible to change people's minds if you understand the local conditions. You can't just pop up out of the blue and tell people what they should and shouldn't do."

"Luckily, people increasingly recognise the need to preserve marine habitats. At the moment, still relatively little of the ocean is protected – or, even if it is, well managed – but we know know that we need to protect 20–40% of it if we are going to stem the loss of biodiversity, protect fish stocks and maintain a healthy balance. The impact of conservation areas quickly becomes obvious. Life returns and local people start to make money from sustainable tourism or see the benefits from spill over it," she explains.

Along with a number of other NGOs, Marshall is campaigning to establish a key protected areas around the globe. Even small LMMAs (Locally Managed Marine Areas) are important and can make a difference to critical habitats, by offering sanctuary to certain species, protecting mating or birthing grounds or maintaining healthy stocks of food for animals Dependant on specific resources.

Local fishermen don't necessarily have to abandon their traditional livelihoods or move away. It may mean a shift in what they fish, how they fish or when they fish. Or they may slowly shift to new, more sustainable livelihoods, many of which can be more attractive and less dangerous or taxing than traditional fishing, making it easier to garner local support or buy-in even if it isn't always easy.

On a broader scale, Marshall finds that people think of the current ocean crisis as something they are not particularly connected with or responsible for. Marshall often has to contend with the attitude that there is simply not much that individuals can do when faced with problems of such a huge magnitude. She sometimes finds this frustrating.

"The truth is that there's a whole lot individuals can do. First and foremost, we can become more aware of our own actions and how they impact on nature. We make dozens of choices every day that impact on our oceans, and we need to be more thoughtful in these choices. We as consumers have far greater power than we think. We're surrounded by companies trying to sell us things – the real revelation comes from the realisation that we drive the market and ultimately they will sell us what we ask for and what we choose to buy."

With a growing family to support, the advantages of a stable job, secure income and a permanent base in a more developed country may be tempting, but Marshall is in Barra to stay.

"My husband and I are committed to this coastline, and we are building a passionate team to become the next generation of ocean ambassadors for Mozambique. It might be hard, and I do sometimes worry about how sustainable this kind of life is, but there is also a deep satisfaction in doing something that you're passionate about and knowing that your efforts will help drive much needed change in a region. At the end of the day, this is what matters most – or at least to me."

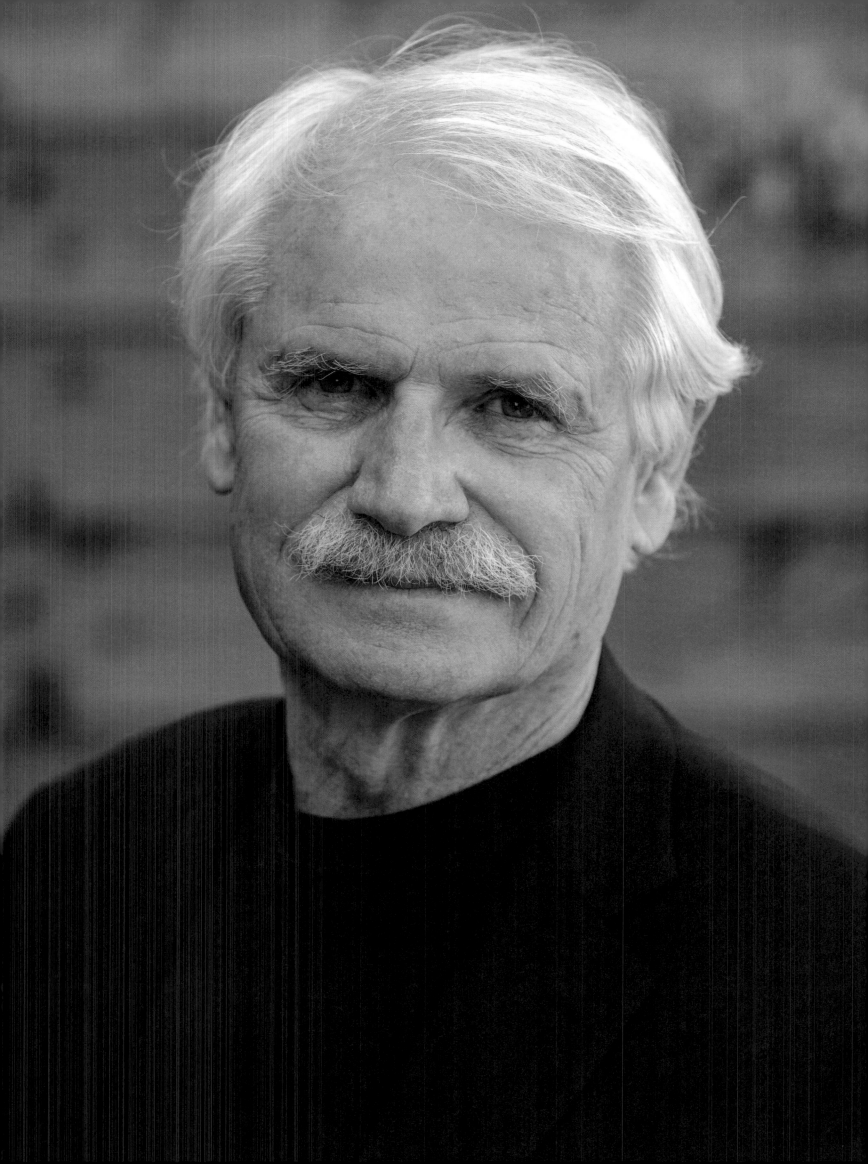

GOAL 15

- -

LIFE ON LAND

- -

"I HAVE SEEN A LOT OF THIS PLANET THAT IS OUR HOME FROM ABOVE, AND IT IS STUNNINGLY BEAUTIFUL.

So many verdant forests, breathtaking coasts and plains, majestic mountains, the myriad of people, animals, insects, plants – the diversity of nature is awe-inspiring.
But I have also seen how we wreck it, overexploit it and take it for granted. I take pictures of the ruin as a warning.
I take pictures of the beauty to inspire us to protect it.
Both are necessary, you cannot protect what you do not love.
Earth deserves to be loved"

YANN ARTHUS-BERTRAND

Environmentalist, activist, film director and photographer,
UNEP Goodwill Ambassador

Previous double page: Agricultural landscape between Ankara and Hattusha, Anatolia, Turkey
(40° 00' N – 33° 35' E)

GOAL 15
PROTECT, RESTORE AND PROMOTE SUSTAINABLE USE OF TERRESTRIAL ECOSYSTEMS, SUSTAINABLY MANAGE FORESTS, COMBAT DESERTIFICATION, STOP AND REVERSE LAND DEGRADATION, AND HALT THE LOSS OF BIODIVERSITY

The vision: By 2030 all terrestrial and inland freshwater ecosystems will be conserved, restored and used sustainably. Deforestation will be halted, and reforestation will be increased substantially. Significant efforts will be made to combat desertification, and degraded land and soil will be restored. Threatened species will have been saved from extinction, and urgent and significant action will have halted the loss of biodiversity. There will be global support for efforts to combat the trafficking and poaching of protected species

FORESTS FOR ALL

10 COUNTRIES ARE HOME TO MORE THAN TWO THIRDS OF THE WORLD'S GLOBAL FOREST COVER

(**Source:** World Bank: SDG Atlas, 2018)

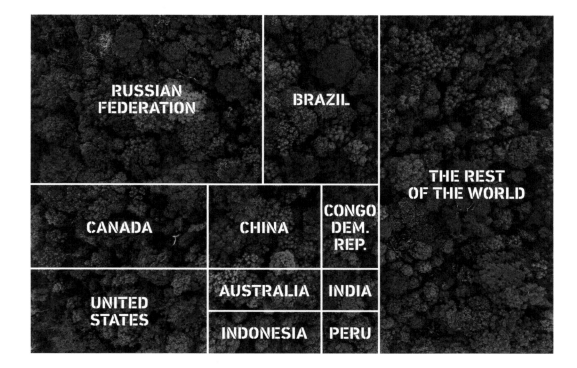

RUSSIAN FEDERATION

BRAZIL

THE REST OF THE WORLD

CANADA

CHINA

CONGO DEM. REP.

UNITED STATES

AUSTRALIA

INDIA

INDONESIA

PERU

A HOME, A DIY STORE, A PHARMACY, A LARDER...

Forests are so much more than just collections of trees. They are the richest of terrestrial ecosystems. Eight out of ten land-based species are reliant on natural forests. The massive variation in habitats provides homes for all sorts of life forms – from microscopic fungi and insects to huge elephants and bears.

Nor is dependency on forests unique to these species. For more than 1.5 billion people, particularly the world's poorest, forests are a home, a DIY store, a larder, a pharmacy and much more besides. They provide fuel, building materials, food and – for up to 80% of people in rural areas in the developing world – medicine too. Yet we have barely started to tap into the potential of forests to supply us with new medicines, despite knowing full well that many existing ones were originally derived from plants.

Forests are also sources of clean water, they prevent soil from turning arid, they prevent soil erosion – which protects human settlements from dangerous and devastating landslides – they limit flooding after torrential downpours, stabilise our climate and absorb CO_2.

And yet, despite all this, we continue to cut them down. Felling to make room to grow feed for all of the animals whose meat we eat, felling for firewood and timber, felling for the illegal trade in valuable types of wood – all of these human activities accelerate the deforestation process.

When forests go, habitats for local species go with them. New plantations do not offset the damage caused when old and previously untouched forests are chopped down. When we lose natural variety, we lose many of the things that make forests so valuable.

Fortunately, a number of countries have already demonstrated that it is possible to increase crop yields without deforestation. New sources of energy will also help to save the forests. Although deforestation is still widespread, the pace is slowing, and in some places, forests are even beginning to return to areas previously stripped bare of trees.

15. CREATE
CAI GUO-QIANG

"I AM STILL INTERESTED IN THE UNSEEN SPIRITUALITY. I AM NOW THINKING MORE ABOUT THE EARTH, OUR SURROUNDINGS, AND THE PHYSICAL WORLD"

It is a moment of complete silence and serenity. In a curiously solemn manner, 99 animals bow their heads before a pool of almost perfectly still water, untouched by either wind or waves. The only thing to disturb the mirror-like surface is a single drop of water from the ceiling.

The scene instantly evokes a vision of paradise. It brings to mind the verse in the Bible about the wolf and the lamb grazing together. But you soon start to feel unsettled. Why are all these animals from different continents gathered around the same waterhole? What are predators and their prey doing side by side? Are they dying of thirst? Have they learned to live together amicably? Or will they tear each other apart as soon as they drink their fill, lift their heads and catch sight of one another?

Are they really animals at all, given that they are made of synthetic materials and covered in dyed goatskin? Or are they symbolic representations of human beings and the reality of our existence – the fact that we may be enemies at times, but we also fight to survive together?

The installation *Heritage* by the Chinese artist Cai Guo-Qiang provides ample scope for interpretation but offers no easy answers. His works usually revolve around the spiritual, the divine, the cosmos... but with *Heritage* he has returned, in his own words, to our planet, our heritage – a heritage that we will one day pass on.

Nonetheless, there is a spiritual element here. According to Cai, the work expresses a kind of longing

CAI GUO-QIANG

Chinese contemporary artist, known for his repertoire of large-scale installations and social projects, merging Eastern philosophy with contemporary social issues. Gunpowder is frequently part of his works. **Artworks:** *White Tone*, 2016 (detail). Next page: *Heritage*, 2013.

for the spirituality that is palpable in the ink drawings of the scholars of ancient China, from a time when man lived humbly and in harmony with nature – in sharp contrast to our modern world.

Heritage was inspired by an experience that he had while visiting the tropical Australian island of North Stradbroke.

"As the clear blue waters, the white sandy beaches of Stradbroke Island, and the rich palette of colours on the bottom of Brown Lake took my breath away, I came to realise that this paradise highlighted the serious problems on our planet. Everywhere on Earth should have been just as beautiful."

15. THINK MEAT AND DAIRY THREATEN THE PLANET

IF WE STOPPED EATING MEAT AND DAIRY, MOTHER NATURE WOULD BE ABLE TO RECLAIM 76% OF THE WORLD'S FARMLAND. THIS WOULD BE THE SINGLE MOST EFFECTIVE AND DIRECT MEANS OF PUTTING THE BRAKES ON CLIMATE CHANGE AND REVERSING THE DECLINE IN BIODIVERSITY, SAYS THE RESEARCHER BEHIND THE BIGGEST EVER STUDY OF THE IMPACT OF AGRICULTURE

Nature's biggest problem is lack of space, and the human activity that uses the most is agriculture. But it doesn't have to be that way. We could give up 76% of the land we use to produce food, rewilding a staggering 3.1 billion hectares – an area the size of Russia, Canada and India combined.

How? By replacing the meat and dairy we eat with vegetables, fruits, cereals, seeds, nuts, seaweed and other plant-based foods.

"We knew meat and dairy were both very resource-intensive, but the figure still took us by surprise," said Joseph Poore, a researcher at Oxford University, who worked with the Agroscope research centre in Switzerland on the study of the environmental impact of agriculture.

Published in *Science* in summer 2018, the study is the most comprehensive ever of its kind. Based on input from 40,000 farms and producers across the globe, Poore analysed the data to identify what types of production do the least and greatest damage.

The message was unambiguous: even the least harmful means of producing meat, milk and cheese use more space and cause more pollution than protein or milk from vegetable sources. No other foods put more pressure on nature and the environment than meat and dairy.

"However, there is a huge difference between the meat producers that cause least and most damage," explains Poore. "Some modes of production are 50 times more damaging than others. But in terms of the overall impact on nature, the climate and the environment, it's still far better to replace meat with a plant-based diet, no matter how the meat is produced."

Meat and dairy products are unsustainable for several reasons. The vast majority of livestock destined for slaughter and for dairy farms live in stalls and consume tons of energy-rich fodder, which makes them grow fast, produce high yields and turn a decent profit. Growing all this fodder takes up large amounts of space and water. Vast tracts of tropical forest have been felled to grow feed crops like soy.

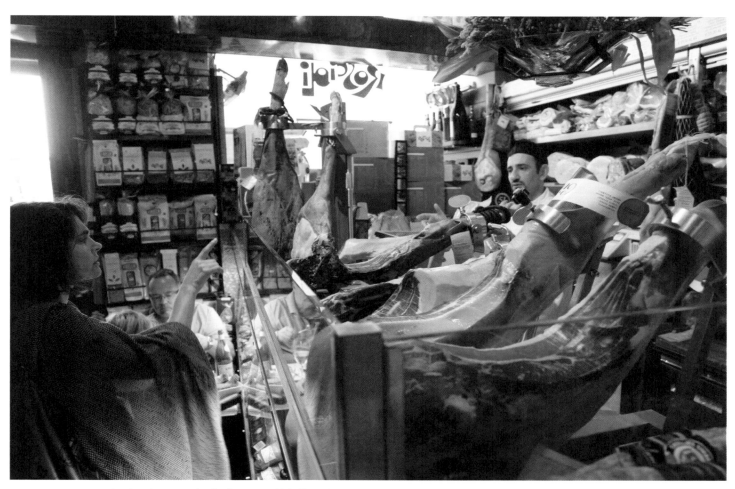

Meat consumption is a danger to both climate and biodiversity. Large areas are deforested to provide fodder and pasture for the animals.

Deforestation not only accelerates climate change but also obliterates plant and animal habitats.

Other habitats on land and in inshore waters are destroyed by fertilisers discharged or seeping into the water, or by air-borne ammonia vapour. Fertiliser may sound like a generally positive thing, but many plants have evolved to survive on scarce nutrition. Artificially fertilising their habitat suffocates and displaces many of these species, which in turn poses a threat to the animals dependent on them. Along coastlines, fertilisers can cause massive algae blooms that consume all of the oxygen in the water, killing fish and shellfish or forcing them to move elsewhere.

The meat producers with the biggest impact on the environment use 370m² of land to produce 100g of protein. It takes only one square metre of crops like beans and peas to produce the same amount of protein. The differences in greenhouse gas emissions are equally startling: some meat producers emit 105kg of CO_2 per 100g of protein, but growing protein-rich plants emits just 0.3kg.

"Another big surprise for us was the size of aquaculture's ecological footprint," says Poore.

Although fish farming doesn't use a large amount of space, it emits a huge amount of methane – a powerful greenhouse gas – and pollutes the environment with fertilisers.

Poore is in no doubt whatsoever. The best thing for our planet right now would be for us to buy significantly less meat – ideally, none at all.

"Unlike many of the other potential measures to address climate change, cutting down on meat and dairy would have a visible effect almost immediately. And we don't have to wait for new legislation. We can just all get on with it and make a difference as individuals," Poore explains.

Cutting meat and dairy production would free up space for nature, for rewilding, for the restoration of habitats on which many species are completely dependent. Organic farming is not enough on its own. More species may thrive in an organically cultivated field than a conventional one – but neither will enjoy anywhere near the levels of biodiversity found in nature. Wild areas are also more resistant to climate change and mitigate the impact of floods, landslides and desertification.

Studies have shown how rapidly nature embraces former agricultural land. As well as adding to natural diversity, the returning trees and bushes help to combat climate change by absorbing CO_2.

Cutting back on meat production would also ease the pressure on valuable water resources – potentially by as much as 25%. In turn, this would lead to less fertiliser discharge, less acidification of both land and sea, and cleaner waterways.

Poore is aware that many people are reluctant to give up meat.

"Even eating half as much and only buying the most sustainably produced meat and dairy would make a big difference. But the problem is that when you're standing in the supermarket, you don't know which products caused the least damage," he says.

"This is where the politicians should step in. We need food-labelling schemes that allow us to make informed choices and better understand how the food we eat affects the environment."

Poore also hopes that the study will increase awareness of the least damaging production methods and allow farmers to learn from one another. He points out that new technology can support sustainability, e.g. by monitoring soil to ensure that crops are watered at optimal intervals and levels and not more than necessary.

"Transparency is the key. Consumers need to know how their food is made and the impact it has on the environment. Informative labelling would also force producers to document what they do, which would increase awareness of sustainability throughout the production chain."

FACTS
• Beef, mutton and pork are the biggest culprits in the meat and dairy sector, while the production of chicken and eggs has the least impact on the environment and climate.

CAN CITIES HELP MAKE THE WORLD A WILDER PLACE?

The immediate outlook may be bleak, but the long-term forecast is really encouraging. Pressure on nature is a phase from which we are about to emerge, and things will look much brighter 100 years down the line, according to a group of researchers led by Eric W. Sanderson, senior conservation ecologist at the American Wildlife Conservation Society.

The prediction is rooted in trends observed in recent decades – especially for migration from rural to urban areas. In brief, the group foresees a short phase of more and more people using more and more resources, after which the population will fall, making room for nature again. The trick is to make sure that nature survives periods when things move in the wrong direction.

Their thinking was set out at length and in detail in a 2018 scientific article entitled "From Bottleneck to Breakthrough". It predicts that a century from now, the global population will be 6–8 billion, extreme poverty will be virtually eliminated, and 70–90% of us will live in towns and cities.

Urban conurbations are the key. Evidence shows that moving to urban areas increases average family income and decreases the number of children. Space is at a premium in cities, so it makes more sense to invest in the education and quality of life of a smaller number of offspring, rather than having many children and struggling to provide for them. In the countryside it makes sense to have more children – space is abundant, and they are a source of cheap labour.

Cities are also more efficient. For example, the researchers point out that the average New Yorker uses 74% less water and 35% less electricity than the average American, and generates 43% less waste.

Cities use very little space, and they use it efficiently. They serve as hubs for innovation, ideas and inventions. Several existing nature conversation organisations were founded in cities, and we can expect even more innovative approaches to conserving species and habitats to emerge from the same circles.

As poverty is eradicated, the population will stabilise then fall, we will all begin to understand the need to protect nature and resources and space will be made for the wild.

So, is the process inevitable? Far from it, the authors admit. If we keep polluting the environment at the current rate, not much nature will be left in 100 years. If we curtail growth and migration to towns and cities as part of nature conservation initiatives, we might not enjoy the affluence and make the breakthroughs needed. But if we strike the right balance between these two extremes, then the situation looks hopeful.

UNINTENDED CONSEQUENCES OF THE HIVE MINDSET

Without butterflies, hoverflies, moths, bees and the like, there would be far fewer species of fruit, vegetables and nuts. Many plants depend on pollinators transferring pollen from flower to flower.

But bees are an endangered species, aren't they? Not all of them. Honey bees aren't, despite the occasional hive collapsing. The widespread misconception that they need to be saved is almost entirely down to a series of campaigns that chose the same symbol – the honey bee.

What the campaigns often overlooked is that honey bees are domesticated, like horses, pigs and sheep. What's more, recent studies show that domestic honey bees actually pose a threat to

wild pollinators and the plant species dependent on them. Bees may be under threat, but it is the wild ones that face extinction, and domestic honey bees are part of the problem.

None of the thousands of species of wild pollinators is as efficient as the honey bee, which flies long distances, works for much of the year and transports huge amounts of pollen. Farmers keep them to pollinate rapeseed fields or orange groves. Once they've done that, they head for the wild, leaving less food for their wild brethren and other important pollinators, which are then displaced.

Honey bees also carry diseases that can spread to wild insects. Researchers at the International Union for Conservation of Nature say that parasites from honey bees have probably pushed at least one species to the brink.

Despite the evidence, people continue to build hives, including out in the wild, labouring under the misapprehension they are doing nature and biodiversity a good turn. In fact, more hives mean more of a threat to wild species.

Scott Hoffman Black, executive director of the Xerces Society for Invertebrate Conservation – says that we have devoted too much time and energy to the honey bee: "Conserving honey bees to save pollinators is like conserving chickens to save the birds."

15. ACT
KARMA PROTECTS CAMBODIAN TREES

BUN SALUTH HAS DEDICATED HIS LIFE TO CONSERVING THE FORESTS OF HIS NATIVE CAMBODIA. THE BUDDHIST MONK BLESSES IMPORTANT TREES SO THAT ANYBODY FELLING THEM AUTOMATICALLY RUINS THEIR REINCARNATION PROSPECTS

When Cambodians enter Monks Community Forest, they know it's a special place. The biggest and oldest trees have been sanctified by monks swathing them ceremonially in saffron robes, and their sacred nature protects the rest of the forest.

Any tree felled or animal injured in the sacred forest will have just as serious an impact on the culprit's next reincarnation as it would if he had harmed or killed a monk. Respect for the monks and their teachings has led to a sharp drop in illegal felling, which has had a beneficial knock-on effect on all of the many other endangered animal and plant species that inhabit the forest.

Monks Community Forest began with a single monk, the Venerable Bun Saluth, whose renown has now spread far beyond his homeland. The necessity of preserving the forests first dawned on him during a trip to Thailand, where vast swathes of ancient indigenous forest had been wiped out. He was aware that much of the original forest had survived in Cambodia and wanted to keep it that way.

In 2001, he started work on what is now Monks Community Forest – the biggest community forest

in Cambodia, which provides shelter and a source of income for thousands of people. They fish, they collect deadwood for use as timber and firewood, they gather ginger, fruit and fungi, many of which have medicinal properties, to sell at markets. They don't fell trees. They help protect them. At the instigation of Bun Saluth, the local authorities have set up unarmed patrols to prevent illegal felling, which poses a serious threat to all tropical forests.

When asked why he sees it as his calling to protect the forest and the life within it, Bun Saluth refers to Buddha. Buddha was born under a tree in the forest. He meditated under a tree in the forest, he attained enlightenment under a tree in the forest, and he died under a tree in the forest. For Bun Saluth, the forest is the home of Buddha. As a monk and a son of Buddha in a figurative sense, he is duty-bound to protect it.

Bun Saluth walks with his novices in the Monks Community Forest. Bun Saluth protects this forest from loggers, poachers and encroachment and regularly makes patrols to check on it.

PEACE, JUSTICE AND STRONG INSTITUTIONS

"IN A WORLD FILLED WITH INCREASED HATRED, AGGRESSION AND DIVISION, the need to defend and protect the notion of peace has become more important, though even more difficult to achieve. Humanity in its broadest sense must come together in compassion, understanding, generosity, justice and respect for others in order to defend global peace. As Beethoven wrote, one single and vibrant chord stemming from the heart, is the only way forward towards peace in this troubled world. It requires our full strength. Let's change the tone!"

JORGE CHAMINÉ

Baritone, Musician for Peace, recipient of the UNESCO Human Rights Medal.
President of the European Music Centre

Previous double page: Basilica of Our Lady of Peace, Yamoussoukro, Ivory Coast
(6° 49' N – 5° 17' W)

GOAL 16
PROMOTE PEACEFUL AND INCLUSIVE SOCIETIES FOR SUSTAINABLE DEVELOPMENT, ENSURE ACCESS TO JUSTICE FOR ALL, AND BUILD EFFECTIVE, ACCOUNTABLE AND INCLUSIVE INSTITUTIONS AT ALL LEVELS

The vision: By 2030 all forms of violence and deaths related to violence will have been significantly reduced, as will abuse, exploitation, trafficking and all forms of violence against and torture of children. The rule of law will be promoted at both national and international levels, and everyone will have equal access to justice. Corruption in all of its forms will be substantially reduced. Institutions will be effective, accountable and transparent. All individuals will have a legal identity and their fundamental rights will be protected

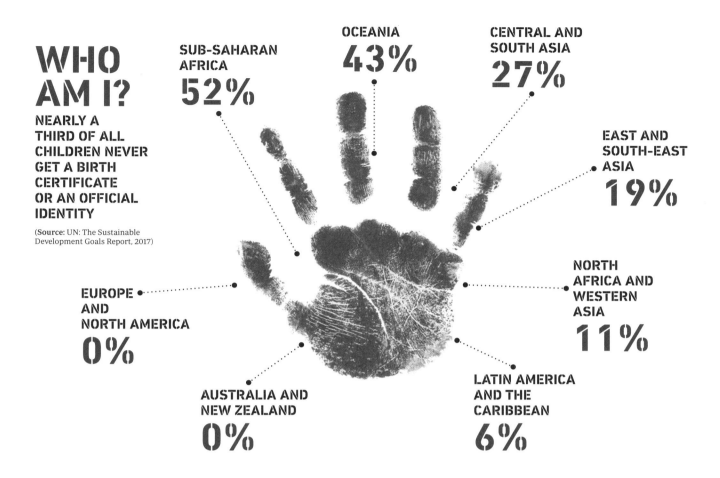

WHO AM I?

NEARLY A THIRD OF ALL CHILDREN NEVER GET A BIRTH CERTIFICATE OR AN OFFICIAL IDENTITY

(**Source:** UN: The Sustainable Development Goals Report, 2017)

SUB-SAHARAN AFRICA
52%

OCEANIA
43%

CENTRAL AND SOUTH ASIA
27%

EAST AND SOUTH-EAST ASIA
19%

NORTH AFRICA AND WESTERN ASIA
11%

EUROPE AND NORTH AMERICA
0%

AUSTRALIA AND NEW ZEALAND
0%

LATIN AMERICA AND THE CARIBBEAN
6%

THE UNIDENTIFIED BILLION

In most of the technologically advanced nations, some form of personal identification is taken for granted. Be it passports, ID cards or tax numbers/codes, different countries identify their citizens in different ways. Possessing official ID is seen as an essential prerequisite to individual empowerment and participation in society in a wider sense. It is used when we vote, open bank accounts and access things like medical care, education and social services.

But over one billion people, at least one in seven of the world's population, have no form of personal ID. They are excluded from a wide range of rights and opportunities – with women suffering disproportionately. In some countries, other minorities and vulnerable groups also have difficulty obtaining official ID.

Ensuring that every citizen has the right to personal ID is a crucial element in the fight against poverty, hunger and inequality. The simple fact of having a bank account makes it safer and easier to receive payments, start a business, operate over distances, access funding and save for the future.

A national programme in Pakistan issued the most vulnerable citizens with ID and bank accounts into which financial aid is deposited. An evaluation of the programme has shown that direct access to their own money has endowed poor Pakistani women with higher local status in their local communities, as well as greater freedom and independence. And now they can vote, too.

ID systems are costly and challenging. Many people live in remote areas, and it takes a lot of time and resources to develop a national register that is secure against abuse and corruption. This is where new technology comes in. Blockchain, which is used by cryptocurrencies like Bitcoin, offers ways of validating identity other than through national records. Used properly, technology has the potential to guarantee permanent and inviolable personal ID, without making individuals dependent on government agencies and their databases. Pilot projects, for example with homeless people in the United States, are already using blockchain as an alternative, but to roll it out on a larger scale would require international collaboration.

16. CREATE
YOKO ONO

"INSTEAD OF THINKING ABOUT DOOMSDAY ALL THE TIME, THINK ABOUT HOW BEAUTIFUL THE WORLD IS. WE'RE ALL TOGETHER, AND TOGETHER WE'RE GETTING WISER" — YOKO ONO

Yoko Ono is an artist who dares to imagine a world of peace and progress. Throughout a career characterised by constant innovation and change, she has retained her faith in love, positivity and the goodness of humankind, ideals she has expressed through music, dance, performance art, film and other art forms.

Her *IMAGINE PEACE* – inspired by the dream she shared with John Lennon of a "Nutopia", a peaceful world without borders – has flown over many cities and adorned billboards, badges, posters and newspaper ads in different languages. The *IMAGINE PEACE TOWER* – a column of light in memory of her late husband and symbolising peace, healing and coexistence – was installed in Iceland in 2007.

Ono was challenging boundaries and unwritten rules long before she met Lennon. And she still is. Her message of peace and of a world without borders is in many ways more provocative today, with nationalism on the rise in several parts of the world, than it was during the flower power era of the '60s and '70s.

Yoko Ono's campaign for peace stems in part from personal, painful experience of the suffering that war brings. The bombing of Japan during the Second World War left her and her family facing starvation. Like so many others, they were forced to beg and

YOKO ONO

Japanese multimedia artist, singer, songwriter, and peace activist, also known for her work in performance art and filmmaking.
Artworks: *IMAGINE PEACE:* as part of Creative Time's *Pledges of Allegiance*, 2017, and *IMAGINE PEACE TOWER*, annual October 9th lighting, Videy Island, Reykjavik, Iceland.

barter for food. Millions of Japanese found themselves homeless after the war, and an unknown number died of starvation.

For many years, Yoko Ono has included Wish Trees in her exhibitions: everybody is invited to write their wishes and hang them on the trees or send them to the wishing well at the *IMAGINE PEACE TOWER*. Sometimes, these trees have blossomed into whole forests of wishes – and over a million of them have made their way to the tower in Iceland.

"If you're busy imagining peace, you can't be killing. That can only be a good thing, right?" — Yoko Ono.

16. THINK
USING BLOCKCHAIN, BIG DATA AND TRANSPARENCY TO COMBAT CORRUPTION

NEW TECHNOLOGIES SUCH AS BLOCKCHAIN AND BIG DATA COULD HELP CURB CORRUPTION, WHICH IS A HUGE BURDEN ON BOTH PEOPLE AND SOCIETIES

Corruption has been dubbed public enemy no. 1 in the developing countries. The World Economic Forum estimates that it eats up 5% of global annual revenue (around $2.6 trillion). According to the World Bank, individuals and companies pay out around $1 trillion p.a. in bribes. And neither figure takes account of sexual extortion, which is such a massive blight on the lives of women and girls in particular.

Corruption isn't just an economic issue. Studies have revealed links between high levels of corruption and high mortality rates. Corruption sometimes prevents poor people from accessing health care, education and other human rights, and in countries where bribery is used to buy votes and jobs, people on low incomes are excluded from influential positions in politics and business.

Corruption thrives in the shadows, but new digital tools like blockchain, big data, open data, and digital self-service are shining a light on its darkest corners. The tools may be very different, but they share certain features:

• They cut out middlemen, which reduces the potential for corruption. Fewer human hands are involved when people enter their own information. Blockchain enables people to send all sorts of data directly – from money to title deeds and contracts – without using banks or other central agencies as a conduit. Electronic voting, as implemented in Estonia for example, makes it pointless to try to bribe officials to tamper with results.

• They enhance transparency. Blockchain data is accessible to anyone who is part of the network – this is what makes it almost impossible to edit data without the agreement of the entire network. Open data – local and national agencies making all data available online – facilitates analyses and detection of irregularities, e.g. if too many procurement contracts are going to the same companies.

• They identify patterns. When large amounts of data are acquired and analysed, e.g. by using artificial intelligence, previously invisible patterns that exclude certain groups from influence and promote corruption become discernible, and this information can be used to develop better policies and expose corrupt ways of working together, such as cartels.

Crowdsourcing and whistleblowing platforms enable people to report bribery and extortion via a website or app. The Indian platform ipaidabribe.com has become particularly popular and has spread to many other countries. Other platforms send anonymous tips to specially chosen media outlets and investigative journalists to expose corruption.

But digital tools only go so far. They only work when combined with the political will to tackle corruption, and they have their own inherent dangers – it's particularly difficult to strike the right balance between the public's right to transparency and the individual's right to privacy. Nor should we forget that data and algorithms can also be used to undermine democracy, as witnessed during the 2016 US presidential election.

DATA AS PEACEKEEPER

The fact that goal 16 is one of the most challenging and difficult to quantify has encouraged various organisations to band together in the UN 2030 Goal 16 Data Initiative, which aims to collect all available data from both official and unofficial sources.

The aim is to produce statistics and definitions that show whether or not the world is on the right track and draw attention to gaps in our knowledge that need to be filled or challenges that need more attention.

The initiative has identified 23 factors so far – interim targets and indicators – that say something about whether society is becoming more or less peaceful and fair – including data on domestic violence, sexual assault, the effectiveness of legal systems, rates of imprisonment without trial and illegal cash flows.

Ultimately, the organisations involved in the initiative hope that national and international organisations and agencies will collate and publish the data instead. In the meantime, they seek to fill a huge data gap, in part by drawing on civil society.

CAN BLOCKCHAIN SAVE THE INVISIBLE CHILDREN?

With no birth certificate and no formal ID, 600 million children under the age of 14 are effectively invisible, leaving them extremely vulnerable to traffickers, who sell them into prostitution and slavery, use them to make fraudulent benefit claims and harvest their organs.

UNICEF estimates that around 1.2 million children are trafficked and exploited each year. Thousands of children from Nepal alone, often as young as eight or nine, are sold into prostitution in India. Many of them don't make it to adulthood, dying from conditions like HIV and lack of health care.

Children without ID are the easiest targets. Criminals use forged documents and false information about age and nationality to smuggle them across borders. Blockchain could be the key to changing this. UN organisations are teaming up with countries with a history of child trafficking (e.g. Moldova) and blockchain specialists to try to protect these invisible children. One potential solution is an ID linked via blockchain to at least two parents or guardians. Fingerprints or iris scans would reveal the true identities of unaccompanied children when they arrive at borders, making it possible to contact their families.

A system like this would not save every vulnerable child. The practicalities need to be ironed out, and sometimes it is the families who traffic the children. Nevertheless, the UN hopes that blockchain ID will go some way toward combating what it terms "one of the greatest human rights abuses."

16. ACT

ZAINAB SALBI: RESISTANCE IN THE FACE OF FEAR

Zainab Salbi, founder of Women for Women, rallies participants before a peace march across the Brooklyn Bridge, New York, USA.

"WE HAVE A CHOICE. WE CAN CHOOSE FEAR AND ANGER. OR WE CAN CHOOSE TO STAND BY OUR IDEALS, TO FIGHT FOR THEM, AND TO CONTINUE TO SPREAD HOPE"

ZAINAB SALBI, HUMANITARIAN, MEDIA HOST, AUTHOR, FOUNDER AND FORMER CEO OF WOMEN FOR WOMEN INTERNATIONAL

She still remembers the fear – the oppressive, all-embracing presence that defined her childhood and youth. Zainab Salbi grew up, quite literally, in the shadow of the Iraqi dictator Saddam Hussein – and sometimes in the light cast by his sunshine. "Uncle Saddam", as the family called him, could be cruel, and sometimes kind, but always unpredictable.

Salbi's father was the Iraqi despot's personal pilot. The whole family knew that they were being watched, that invisible ears were listening to their every conversation. Fear poisoned her family's life, making it impossible to think or speak freely.

She remembers the fear when she gave in to her mother's tears and pressure and agreed to marry a man and move with him to America. She remembers the fear as he raped her. She remembers the fear, when, as a 19-year-old, she fled her marriage and set off into the unknown with just a few hundred dollars to her name.

She was an immigrant in a country she hardly knew and felt betrayed by her parents for putting her in a marriage in a strange land, cut off from Iraq by the first Gulf War. Later, she would learn that her family's fear of Saddam had been the motivation behind the arranged marriage, but for many years she had no contact with them and was still afraid of the dictator, despite living on another continent.

Saddam is now dead, and Zainab Salbi is frequently cited as one of the most influential women in the world. She has been awarded prizes for her work on behalf of women, peace and justice. She travels the world and appears on talk shows – but fear is still part of her life.

She no longer fears for herself, but for the future of the ideals that underpin freedom and democracy. She is worried about the fear that dominates political debate in many parts of the world.

"Fear is a bad leader. We make bad decisions when we let it guide us. It is beginning to undermine Western values – we are willing to sacrifice them because we are afraid. Afraid of immigration, afraid of unemployment, afraid of the future."

"But if we fight that fear by abandoning our values, we start to fight ourselves. People are forever saying that we need to defend ourselves and what we stand for. But if that means abandoning human rights and restricting freedoms, then we've already lost everything that defines us. We lose ourselves, we lose our soul, we lose the moral authority to promote those ideals."

Despite her difficult start, Salbi managed to build a life for herself in the USA. She learned about the meaning of freedom and the history of democracy, gradually coming to the realisation that she now lived in a place where she could choose, that she was no longer at the mercy of the whims and desires of others. She was no longer powerless.

Soon after, she met the Palestinian-American lawyer Amjad Atallah, who would become her second husband. Their honeymoon was unique. It was the height of the civil war in then Yugoslavia. Salbi and Atallah had read about the plight of the Bosnian women in rape camps, who had lost their whole families to ruthless ethnic cleansing. The young couple decided to go there and help.

It marked the beginning of Zainab's life as an activist. She asked other women for financial help to support women in Bosnia and set up the Women for Women International network. To date, the organisation has provided more than $100 million in aid to victims of war throughout the world, but according to Salbi the money and practical aid are not the only important forms of support.

"We were also able to tell the women that they hadn't been forgotten. That people cared about them. We offered them hope. It's more difficult now. What am I supposed to say to people trying to escape brutal wars, people who, in our fear, we try to prevent fleeing to safety? The West has promoted its ideals of freedom and justice far and wide, values for which millions have fought and even died. So when the West starts to abandon those very ideals, it extinguishes the light of hope for others. What am I supposed to say? 'Yes, you're right. You've been forgotten. Nobody wants to take you in and protect you, the rest of the world is busy with all sort of other issues.'"

Salbi believes that the West's risk of betrayal of its own principles is far more significant than we realise. Many people no longer feel they can rely on the West and are seeking alliances elsewhere. This leaves a huge power vacuum on the global political stage – and we don't yet know who will fill it or what values they will espouse.

"Certain forces are driven by a kind of hunger. It's not about good and evil, but about having had so little

that now all you want to do is take, take, take," she says.

In her darkest moments, Salbi admits that it would be easy to be engulfed by pessimism. But she chooses not to. And it is, indeed, a choice. As the title of her book puts it, "freedom is an inside job". If you crumble in the face of fear, you might as well put on your own chains. But she also sees hope, not least in the #MeToo movement, which has given women across the world a voice and a platform to tell and take ownership of their own stories.

She has also found hope in the almost obliterated Iraqi city of Mosul. Almost everything is gone – schools, roads, houses, mosques, churches. At the end of their long battle against ISIS, the people of the city were consumed with anger and the desire for revenge. But when Salbi visited them, she encountered a community shocked by its own reactions.

"They told me that they had turned into ticking time bombs. They had abandoned everything they believed in. They discovered that it isn't possible to build a society based on anger, fear and revenge – it takes dialogue, forgiveness and compassion. 'We need new ideals, we need to build a new type of human being,' they said. It is important that we listen to them. These are people who know what it means to betray what you stand for," says Salbi.

"We have a choice. We can choose fear and anger. Or we can choose to stand by our ideals, to fight for them, and to continue to spread hope. We need leadership that relies on tools other than fear, and that has to begin within us. Look at me: I am a woman of colour, a Muslim, an immigrant, and I endured dictatorship, exile, an arranged marriage, and poverty. If I can do it, anybody can."

17 PARTNERSHIPS
FOR THE GOALS

PARTNERSHIPS FOR THE GOALS

"I HAVE ALWAYS BEEN A STRONG BELIEVER THAT BUSINESS MUST FIRST AND FOREMOST SERVE SOCIETY. Our current form of capitalism is leaving too many people behind. The Sustainable Development Goals have given us a road map to reboot the future and change the way society and thereby businesses function. It is our moral obligation to do everything we can to achieve these goals, but it also makes good business sense. There is, after all, no business case for enduring poverty"

PAUL POLMAN
Unilever CEO 2009–2018. Chair ICC. SDG Advocate

Previous double page: Meeting in a stadium, west Seoul, Gyeonggy, South Korea
(37° 34′ N – 126° 53′ E)

GOAL 17 IMPROVE IMPLEMENTATION AND REVITALISE THE GLOBAL PARTNERSHIP FOR SUSTAINABLE DEVELOPMENT

The vision: By 2030 developed countries will have fully implemented their official commitment to development assistance. Internationally, there will be greater sharing of knowledge and technology, and developing countries will gain access to environmentally sound technologies on favourable terms. Their exports will have increased, and the share of global exports among the least developed countries will have doubled. Global partnerships for sustainable development, expertise, technology and financial resources will be enhanced, as will public-private and civil society partnerships

DEVELOPMENT ASSISTANCE HAS DOUBLED

(**Source:** UN: The Sustainable Development Goals Report, 2017)

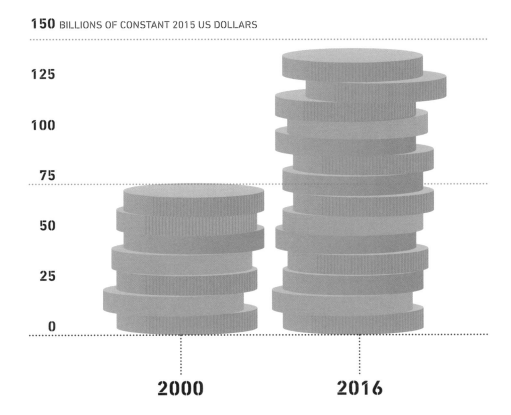

150 BILLIONS OF CONSTANT 2015 US DOLLARS

125

100

75

50

25

0

2000   **2016**

NEW ALLIANCES NEEDED

At both formal and informal summits and conferences, two large groups have long since taken up what many see as their natural place alongside our political leaders: the business community and civil society (a blanket term covering formal and informal networks of NGOs, activists, artists, and civic and interest groups).

Sometimes, both of these groups are seen as little more than lobbying organisations intent on influencing politicians to make decisions in a way that suits their own narrow interests. However, as far as the UN 2030 Goals are concerned, they are so much more than that. They are partners in the process, indispensable ones. Nations may still be the main drivers behind the global agenda, but business and civil society have proven themselves capable of getting things done and producing new knowledge, possibilities and solutions.

Granted, these alliances may at times be uneasy. Civil society groups are often highly critical of both government and business, and they do not always

receive the warmest of welcomes at the table. In some countries, civil engagement is tantamount to putting your life on the line. In others, political and business leaders dismiss criticism from such groups as unfair and overly simplistic.

Similarly, the business community is often accused of only being interested in profit. The reality is different. More and more business leaders are seizing the 2030 agenda as an opportunity not just to make money, but also to develop solutions to some of the biggest problems faced by the world today.

Nonetheless, there is an increasing understanding and acceptance of the fact that the 17 UN Sustainable Development Goals will not be achieved by politicians alone. Yes, political leadership is necessary, but we also need critical voices, civic engagement and the business community's capacity for innovative solutions. We need a commitment that transcends geographical, economic and social boundaries. Only by working in partnership will we meet the UN 2030 Goals.

17. CREATE
WANGECHI MUTU

"THESE CONSERVATIVE DEMARCATIONS OF NATION AND STATE AND CULTURE ARE SOON GOING TO BE ARCHAIC. WE HAVE TO REDEFINE WHAT WE MEAN WHEN WE SAY: 'WHO ARE YOUR PEOPLE?' 'WHERE ARE YOU FROM?'"

We have never been more connected. At the touch of a button, we communicate in real time across continents and time zones. We look each other in the eye as we speak, despite being thousands of miles apart. We share our views and our lives on social media with close friends and strangers alike.

Technology enables us to work together with more people, and in more ways, than ever before. And yet, according to Wangechi Mutu, we have never been more divided. *A Promise to Communicate* aims to rectify that by creating a space where communication flows freely. The centrepiece of the installation consists of a giant world map – but not as we know it from school. Continents and countries have drifted apart, found new neighbours and changed size and shape.

The landmasses are made of recycled blankets used by emergency aid organisations, refugee camps and air-sea rescue teams. No people appear on the map, only the blankets they used. It serves as a reminder of the fact that we don't communicate with one another, we don't see, don't listen, don't reach out – even though we could. The flow of suffering people is a global issue and will only be solved by working together – and yet we are just as far apart from each other as the countries on Mutu's map.

The public is invited to write on the wall beneath the folded blankets. It is covered with poetry, peace

WANGECHI MUTU

Contemporary artist known primarily for her painting, sculpture, film and performance work. Born in Kenya, she has lived and established her career in New York. **Artwork:** *A Promise to Communicate*, 2018.

symbols, drawings of handshakes and words of solidarity. It is a space in which to communicate, and people are making the most of it. Although she now lives and works in New York, Wangechi Mutu was born in Kenya, and African culture plays a major role in her work. Working with diverse and multi-layered approaches, and a wide range of idioms – including collage, painting, performance, video and sculpture – she gets to the heart of questions of gender, identity, race and social injustice.

17. THINK THE FUTURE IS OURS TO SHAPE

POLITICIANS, SCIENTISTS, OTHER EXPERTS, NGOS AND THE PRIVATE SECTOR ALL HAVE AN IMPORTANT PART TO PLAY IN THE RUN-UP TO 2030. WE ALL DO – EVERY LAST ONE OF US

A world free from poverty, hunger, and disease. A world in which all life forms thrive. Taken together, the UN 2030 Goals provide the framework for this vision of the future.

A simple concept perhaps, but also pretty overwhelming – especially in the face of the daily deluge of unsettling and tragic news dished up by the media. Although the nations of the world have signed up to this vision for 2030, the politicians often leave much to be desired when it comes to leadership. A large and growing number of companies may proclaim their commitment to sustainability at every level, but other persistent and cynical polluters still operate all over the world. The fact that academic institutions and researchers don't always agree on causes, effects and solutions, and that NGOs often compete for attention, only compounds matters and makes it tricky to determine priorities.

All of these difficulties make it tempting to just give up. But responsibility for the UN 2030 Goals begins with the individual. We don't have to wait for politicians, experts, business leaders or grassroots movements to make a difference.

Goal 17 is all about partnerships – indeed, the overarching global partnership is crucial to making the vision a reality – and we all have a role to play. The 169 sub-targets provide inspiration for ideas and action, both as individuals and in the public and professional spheres.

We can support organisations, companies and leaders whom we trust and whose work we value. We can share our knowledge. We can inspire others. We can help in our local communities – either by volunteering or simply by helping neighbours, vulnerable children, young people and the more elderly.

Each of the UN's goals embraces a multitude of possibilities. Thousands of actions, big and small, would make a difference and help bring us a little closer to the future to which we aspire.

CONTRIBUTE FROM THE COMFORT OF YOUR HOME

- **SAVE ELECTRICITY** and switch off everything you're not using. Remember – standby mode burns energy. Use LEDs and other energy-saving forms of lighting.
- **DON'T PRINT.** If you want to remember something, make a digital note, e.g. a bookmark in your browser.
- **EXERT INFLUENCE.** Demand that official agencies make sustainable decisions at local, national and international level.
- **IF YOU SPOT ONLINE BULLYING, REPORT IT.**

THINGS TO DO IN YOUR HOME

- **HANG OUT YOUR CLOTHES** – and hair! – to dry. It saves energy.
- **TAKE SHORT SHOWERS.** A bath uses far more water than a five-minute shower.
- **CUT DOWN ON MEAT, FISH AND DAIRY.** Plant-based products burn up far fewer resources.
- **RECYCLE** as much as possible and generate as little waste as possible.
- **AVOID SINGLE-USE PLASTICS** – straws, single-use cups, plastic cutlery, etc.
- **INSULATE YOUR HOME** so that it uses as little energy as possible for heating or air-conditioning.

THINGS TO DO IN YOUR LOCAL COMMUNITY

- **SHOP LOCALLY.** It keeps businesses and shops going, creates jobs and reduces pollution from transport.
- **ONLY EAT SUSTAINABLY SOURCED SEAFOOD.** Let local restaurants and shops know that sustainability is important to you.
- **WALK, CYCLE OR USE PUBLIC TRANSPORT.** If you do drive, car pool.
- **DRIVE SAFELY.** Every year, more than 1.3 million people die in traffic accidents – it is the leading cause of death among children and young people.
- **ALWAYS TAKE A BAG WHEN YOU GO SHOPPING** – don't buy single-use ones. Even paper bags harm the environment. The most sustainable option is a canvas bag-for-life.
- **USE SECOND-HAND STORES** and recycling schemes. If you don't need it any more, pass it on or donate it to a good cause.
- **EXERCISE YOUR DEMOCRATIC RIGHTS.** Register to vote, join a political organisation or stand for election.

THINGS TO DO AT YOUR WORK

- **HELP YOUNGER COLLEAGUES** – volunteer to mentor. It's a good way to help others make progress.
- **STAND UP FOR EQUAL PAY AND EQUAL RIGHTS** in the workplace.
- **DO YOUR BIT** to make sure that your workplace is sustainable and operates ethically at both local and global levels.
- **SPEAK UP IF YOU WITNESS DISCRIMINATION** or harassment. We are all equal, irrespective of race, gender, sexual orientation, religion, social background or disability.

17. ACT

JAN ELIASSON:
THE MOST IMPORTANT
WORD TODAY IS
"TOGETHER"

Jan Eliasson has visited multiple war zones
and refugee camps during his life. Here he greets
the children at a school for Syrian child refugees
in northern Beirut in Lebanon.

"ALL STATES HAVE A ROLE TO PLAY AT INTERNATIONAL LEVEL BY BUILDING HEALTHY, SAFE, SECURE AND SUSTAINABLE SOCIETIES, BUT THEY CANNOT ISOLATE THEMSELVES IF WE ARE TO BUILD A BETTER FUTURE"

JAN ELIASSON, FORMER DEPUTY SECRETARY GENERAL OF THE UN, AND CURRENT CHAIR OF THE STOCKHOLM INTERNATIONAL PEACE RESEARCH INSTITUTE

Many years ago, when still young and unknown in politics and diplomacy, which would go on to make him a key player on the world stage, Eliasson had to make an important speech. He remembers being nervous. "I don't know what to say," he confided in his mother, in their working-class home in the Swedish city of Gothenburg.

"Just tell them what's in your heart," she advised. The young Eliasson did just that – and has kept on doing so. It's a heart filled with a burning desire to make the world a better place, one where human rights and dignity are respected, where there are enough resources for everyone – including future generations – and where war and conflict no longer cause great suffering and death.

As a worldview, it sounds at one and the same time a bit banal and infinitely ambitious, just like both the

2030 Sustainable Development Goals and the 2015 Millennium Development Goals before them. Eliasson has been a driving force behind the two, especially when he was Deputy Secretary General of the United Nations from 2012 to 2016. The two sets of goals have a great deal in common, but he also points out that there are significant differences.

"The 2015 goals were specifically aimed at developing countries. Enormous progress was made, and many of the objectives were met. The 2030 goals are global. In a sense, they treat all countries like developing ones," explains Eliasson, who currently is the chair of the governing board of the renowned Stockholm International Peace Research Institute, SIPRI.

At one point, he and his colleagues tried to sum up the 17 global goals in a single sentence.

"We started off with 'a roadmap to a sustainable future' but weren't entirely happy with it and went back to the drawing board. Next, we came up with 'a toolbox to save the world'. Then, we agreed on 'a survival kit for humanity', and it stuck because it accurately conveys what the goals are all about and implies that achieving them will require a great deal of goodwill and effort," he recalls.

The partnerships envisaged in UN 2030 Goal 17 aren't restricted to wealthy countries helping the world's poorest nations and people, although this is something to which Eliasson is deeply committed. As president of the UN General Assembly in the mid-2000s, he liked to propose toasts to clean water, reminding those present that access to clean drinking water is a privilege – and one that hundreds of millions of people still don't enjoy, despite all the progress humanity has made.

Goal 17 is about involving everyone – from politicians and the private sector to civil society and academia – in the campaign to realise the vision of a better future articulated in the 2030 goals. Eliasson sees both threats and opportunities.

"I'm impressed by the private sector and business world. They've really embraced the goals and understand what's at stake. Civil society is brimming with initiatives and committed individuals who are constantly campaigning. It's all very heartening," he says.

On the other hand, he hopes to see greater engagement from the academic world. "We need our universities and research institutions to get more involved if we are to solve the huge challenges of guaranteeing food for all, slowing climate change and preserving the Earth's resources. We need them to play a bigger part if we are to make the big breakthroughs required," Eliasson explains.

He adds an appeal to the media for help, claiming that the "shocking lack of knowledge" about the 2030 goals is at least partly their responsibility. They are failing to inform and engage with their audiences

Eliasson is also concerned by current political trends, especially the rise of populism and nationalism in countries where human rights have underpinned democracy for more than half a century.

"We are seeing countries withdraw from binding international partnerships and agreements because of concerns raised at home. But challenges like migration, working conditions, climate change, the depletion of natural resources, pollution and the economy can't be addressed in isolation at a national level. The border between the national and the international is blurring," says Eliasson.

However, he is quick to emphasise that this doesn't make the role of the nation subordinate.

"Working at a national level to create healthy, inclusive and sustainable societies also helps build a better world. We need to build societies with solid and fair welfare systems and respect for human rights because by making your own country peaceful, safe and fair you make an important contribution to global peace and security."

Peace and security are key elements of Eliasson's current role and run like a red thread through most of his international work. As a diplomat, he has helped to mediate some of the world's most horrific conflicts, including in Sudan, Iran and Iraq. As Sweden's foreign minister, and in his various UN roles, he has seen war and the suffering it causes first-hand.

Eliasson emphasises that there is an undeniable two-way causal link between violent conflicts and other global issues.

"Wars and violence are often about resources – lack of water and food, for example – but it's a vicious and self-perpetuating cycle," says Eliasson, pointing to the current situation in Syria, where much of the population is currently suffering food shortages.

In 2017, the civil war in South Sudan led to the UN declaring the first famine in six years. The world may have become better at guaranteeing food security, but wars and conflicts quickly lead to disastrous shortages.

Violence also increases the risk of migration, epidemics, depletion of natural resources and the extinction of animal and plant species. At the same time, climate change can also exacerbate existing conflicts and trigger new ones, for example as a result of flooding or drought.

"That's why the 17 goals are not independent of each other. None of them stands alone – they're interdependent and mutually reinforcing. We can't address climate issues without control of food production. We can't abolish hunger without slowing climate change. We can't secure peace, equality, better health, less poverty and better education without greater fairness. The goals are inextricably linked, and we all have to do our bit to make them happen. 'Together' is the most important word."

HUMAN RIGHTS DECLARATION

THE UNIVERSAL DECLARATION OF HUMAN RIGHTS WAS ADOPTED IN 1948. SINCE THEN TREMENDOUS PROGRESS HAS BEEN MADE, BUT MANY CHALLENGES REMAIN. THE DECLARATION REMAINS OUR BEST HOPE FOR A SECURE, JUST, FREE AND PEACEFUL WORLD. THIS IS A SIMPLIFIED VERSION WRITTEN BY AMNESTY INTERNATIONAL

ARTICLE 1: We are all born free and equal. We all have our own thoughts and ideas. We should all be treated in the same way. **ARTICLE 2:** These rights belong to everybody, whatever our differences. **ARTICLE 3:** We all have the right to life, and to live in freedom and safety. **ARTICLE 4:** Nobody has any right to make us a slave. We cannot make anyone else our slave. **ARTICLE 5:** Nobody has any right to hurt or torture us or treat us cruelly. **ARTICLE 6:** Everyone has the right to be protected by the law. **ARTICLE 7:** The law is the same for everyone. It must treat us all fairly. **ARTICLE 8:** We can all ask for the law to help us when we are not treated fairly. **ARTICLE 9:** Nobody has the right to put us in prison without a good reason, to keep us there or to send us away from our country. **ARTICLE 10:** If we are put on trial, this should be in public. The people who try us should be independent and impartial. **ARTICLE 11:** Nobody should be blamed for doing something until it has been proved. When people say we did a bad thing we have the right to show it is not true. **ARTICLE 12:** Nobody should try to harm our good name. Nobody has the right to come into our home, open our letters, or bother us, or our family, without a good reason. **ARTICLE 13:** We all have the right to go where we want to in our own country and to travel abroad as we wish. **ARTICLE 14:** If we are frightened of being badly treated in our own country, we all have the right to run away to another country to be safe. **ARTICLE 15:** We all have the right to belong to a country. **ARTICLE 16:** Every adult has the right to marry and have a family if they want to. Men and women have the same rights when they are married, and when they are separated. **ARTICLE 17:** Everyone has the right to own things or share them. Nobody should take our things from us without a good reason. **ARTICLE 18:** We all have the right to believe in what we want to believe, to have a religion, or to change it if we wish. **ARTICLE 19:** We all have the right to make up our own minds, to think what we like, to say what we think, and to share our ideas with other people. **ARTICLE 20:** We all have the right to meet our friends and to work together in peace to defend our rights. Nobody can make us join a group if we don't want to. **ARTICLE 21:** We all have the right to take part in the government of our country. Every adult should be allowed to vote to choose their own leaders. **ARTICLE 22:** We all have the right to a home, enough money to live on and medical help if we are ill. Music, art, craft and sport are for everyone to enjoy. **ARTICLE 23:** Every adult has the right to a job, to a fair wage for their work, and to join a trade union. **ARTICLE 24:** We all have the right to rest, and to a break from work . **ARTICLE 25:** We all have the right to enough food, clothing, housing and health care. Mothers and children and people who are old, unemployed or disabled have the right to be cared for. **ARTICLE 26:** We all have the right to education, and to finish primary school, which should be free. We should be able learn a career, or to make use of all our skills. **ARTICLE 27:** We all have the right to our own way of life, and to enjoy the good things that science and learning bring. **ARTICLE 28:** There must be proper order so we can all enjoy rights and freedoms in our own country and all over the world. **ARTICLE 29:** We have a duty to other people, and we should protect their rights and freedoms. **ARTICLE 30:** Nobody can take away these rights and freedoms from us.

- -

According to the independent Danish Institute for Human Rights The 2030 Agenda is explicitly grounded in international human rights treaties. The commitment to human rights is reflected in the general principle of non-discrimination and the aim to "leave no one behind". 156 of the 169 targets have substantial linkages to human rights and labour standards. The UN 2030 Goals and human rights are tied together. Human rights offer guidance for the implementation of the 2030 Agenda, while the goals can contribute substantially to the realisation of human rights.

INDEX

Previous page:
Human Tower Competition in Tarragona, Spain. "Castells" were
declared by UNESCO as one of the Masterpieces of the Oral and Intangible
Heritage of Humanity.

ACKNOWLEDGEMENTS

Maggie Bie, Jill Fritzo, Majken Gilmartin, Greatsimple.com
Hans Gregersen, Marianne Haahr, Pamela Harrington,
Françoise Jacquot, Ulrik Norup Jørgensen, Ray Kurzweil,
Robert Li, Mogens Lykketoft, Gary Mantoosh, Harley Neuman,
Tamela G. Noboa, Catherine Olim,
Anne Poulsen WFP (World Food Programme),
Andreas Malmos Rasmussen, David Risley,
Birgitte and Jim Hagemann Snabe, Jessica Stark, Chuck Thomas,
Shalene Yuen, Jochen Zeitz, Mercedes Zobel

UNDP NORDIC OFFICE, Mette Fjalland
UN Office Geneva: Michael Møller,
Aziyade Louise Poltier Mutal, Michele Zaccheo

Life Exhibitions and **Life Publishing**
were founded in 2001 by Stine Trier Norden and Søren Rud.
Life Exhibitions has a remarkable track record in staging
outdoor photo exhibitions on three main topics: Climate,
Nature and Sustainability. Life Exhibitions operates Life Publishing,
the primary purpose of which is to continuously raise awareness
of the fragile state of our planet. Life Exhibitions also wants to
convey how new, innovative and collaborative approaches to
sustainable action contribute to achieving the 2030 UN Goals.
www.lifeexhibitions.com

Printed by **Tryk Team**, Svendborg, Denmark

This book is produced in accordance with the Nordic Eco-label ("The Swan").
This ensures that strict environmental criteria are met with a restricted
emission of CO_2 in the production of paper, and with only vegetable- and
water-based colour prints used in the printing process. The paper has PEFC
forest certification supporting sustainable forestry.

541 204
tryksag

FSC
www.fsc.org
MIX
Paper from
responsible sources
FSC® C134617

CC-000014/DK